HOW TO READ
MODERN
BUILDINGS

HOW TO READ
MODERN
BUILDINGS

A crash course in the architecture
of the modern era

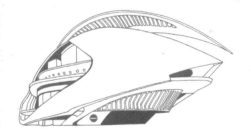

Will Jones

Bloomsbury Visual Arts
An imprint of Bloomsbury Publishing Plc

B L O O M S B U R Y
LONDON · OXFORD · NEW YORK · NEW DELHI · SYDNEY

Bloomsbury Visual Arts

An imprint of Bloomsbury Publishing Plc

Imprint previously known as A&C Black Visual Arts

50 Bedford Square	1385 Broadway
London	New York
WC1B 3DP	NY 10018
UK	USA

www.bloomsbury.com

BLOOMSBURY and the Diana logo are trademarks of Bloomsbury Publishing Plc

First published in Great Britain in 2016 by Bloomsbury Visual Arts

© 2016 Ivy Press Limited

British Library Cataloguing-in-Publication Data

A catalogue record for this book is available from the British Library.

ISBN: 978-1-4742-1903-7

Colour origination by Ivy Press Reprographics

Printed in China

This book was conceived, designed and produced by **Ivy Press**

210 High Street

Lewes, East Sussex

BN7 2NS

UK

www.ivypress.co.uk

CREATIVE DIRECTOR Michael Whitehead

PUBLISHER Susan Kelly

EDITORIAL DIRECTOR Tom Kitch

ART DIRECTOR James Lawrence

EDITOR Jamie Pumfrey

DESIGN JC Lanaway

ILLUSTRATOR Jamie Bush

Contents

Modern buildings are about much more than the white walls, flat roofs and glass-clad skyscrapers that many would class as Modernist. In architectural terms the modern era spans a whole raft of styles and nuances, and encompasses the entire 20th century as well as the early part of the 21st. It takes in possibly the widest variety of styles of any architectural era, from the Renaissance Revival, a reversion to classical form but using the newest industrial methods

of the time, to the glamour of Art Deco, the severity of Brutalism, the quirkiness of the Avant Garde movement – and more.

Modern buildings have evolved so quickly for many reasons. They have been influenced by a socio-political doctrine forced upon nations by economic depression and war. Environmental considerations have come to the fore as we begin fully to understand our impact upon the planet, and, critically, buildings have evolved rapidly because of giant leaps in material technology, construction methods and architectural innovation. In 100 years construction went from relying predominantly on wood and

Classic modern
Grand Central Station (1903–13) looks like a classical building and its aesthetic design is heavily influenced by the French Beaux Arts movement of the 18th and 19th centuries. When completed in 1913 the style was all the rage in the United States.

The mission of *How To Read Modern Buildings* is to introduce these architectural styles and construction techniques, and then investigate them through the different types of building most commonly encountered today. From the homes that we live in to towering skyscrapers, this book will illustrate how each type has been influenced by a progression of modern ideals. We will uncover architectural milestones, iconic landmarks and best-kept secrets from the great age of travel and leisure; we'll delve into religious architecture, industrial and educational buildings; and we'll uncover the key elements that mark a building as a particular modern style.

How To Read Modern Buildings will be the pocket guide to the built environment around you and your crash course in modern architecture with an insight into the array of styles that characterise the places in which you live, work and play.

Inside-out architecture
The Lloyds Building in London (1978–86) is High Tech architecture at its finest. Designed by Richard Rogers, the steel and glass building has its mechanical services on the exterior and superstructure of steel and concrete on show, for all to see.

stone as support structures to embracing steel, reinforced and prestressed concrete, tensile fabrics, structural glass and even plastics. A whole new world of possibilities opened up to designers and builders, and as a result, a plethora of styles developed.

Looking for Clues

Identifying a building's style is often a tricky business. While some buildings have been designed to a rigid doctrine, most are influenced by a number of styles. However, every house, office block and train station has its architectural roots planted somewhere and a well-trained eye can spot the clues – some big, some small – that give the game away. Take these two buildings: the Glass House, far right, is strictly Modernist, its use of steel and glass quickly revealing its style. Mosse House, below, by way of contrast, includes both classical and Art Deco elements in its façade.

Deco redo

Erich Mendelsohn renovated Berlin's Mosse House (1921–23) to combine the classical stone façades (at sides) and a new Art Deco-inspired 'crown'. Note the curved plate glass windows, horizontal banding and 'wings' at the outer edges of the upper stories; all are indicators of Art Deco design.

Same differences

The Crescent Resort Hotel in Miami Beach (1938) wonderfully illustrates the use of asymmetry in the Art Deco genre; the front façade includes classic decorative themes and colours, put to great use in a fun and stylish design.

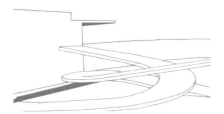

Classic quirks

The Penguin Pool at London Zoo (1934) was designed by Berthold Lubetkin. Its combination of a minimal material palette – concrete – and playful form indicate that it is an early Modernist design. The cantilevered, curved ramps are extremely sophisticated engineering and the pool is now Heritage-listed.

Making Modern

The severity of design in Philip Johnson's Glass House (1949) marks it as a building born of a new era. Glass and steel, and little else, no unnecessary adornments and a rigid rectilinear footprint: the roots of the Modernist genre are laid out in this simple, beautiful design.

Redefining the norm

This Croatian house (2012), designed by AVP Arhitekti + SANGRAD, redefines the classical ideal of a home, taking the archetypal form and elevating it over a Modernist white box. The result is a combination that is at once both understandable and challenging.

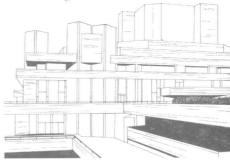

Getting brutal

The Royal National Theatre (1969–76), London, is an example of Brutal architecture. The severe concrete form is termed brutal not due to its looks but to the French term *béton brut* or 'raw concrete'. Needless to say, the name defines the genre.

Introduction

Modernist icon
Perhaps the most famous Modernist house in the world, Villa Savoye (1928–31), designed by Le Corbusier, exemplifies many of the traits of the mid-century style. While it is an unusual shape when compared to conventional homes, every aspect is designed with function in mind.

The question of style is a big one in the modern era because in this period architecture seemed to morph almost constantly from one style to another. This swift movement between architectural ideals and philosophies has seen architects more apt to mix and combine styles in order to achieve the 'perfect' building design. That said, an architect has usually been schooled in a particular genre and the founding tenets of the style will be evident in every design. Our task is to begin to understand some of the thinking behind the decisions that make a building and so decipher its style and the meaning behind the bricks, mortar, steel or stone.

In this first section of *How To Read Modern Buildings* we will take a look at the predominant styles of the 20th century, investigating them in the order in which they took centre stage on the architectural scene. Initially, we'll check out the outgoing classically inspired genres of Renaissance Revival and Beaux Arts, before moving on to the years after the First World War and the rise of Art Deco glamour.

Even while Art Deco was at the peak of its popularity there were 'designs' afoot to take architecture in a new direction. And, while masterpieces such as New York City's gilded jewel, the Chrysler Building, were still in construction architects in Europe were plotting a Modernist revolution.

And so the story unfolds, from early Modernism and Europe's Bauhaus movement to the International School, the United States' answer to the social leanings of architects across the Pond. Combining the two, Modernism took root, only to be usurped (to some extent) in the 1970s by the Postmodernists, a group of architects who eschewed the 'form follows function' mantra of their peers.

And in the midst of these monumental shifts in architectural thinking we should not forget the fringe factions: the Expressionists, Futurism, Art Nouveau, the Avant Garde and Minimalism. Each style has its defining markers and this grammar of styles will give a good grounding in what we need to look out for as we uncover the architectural stories of modern buildings.

Broadcasting House in London

Home of the BBC, this Art Deco building (1928–32) in London was designed by architects George Val Myer and Raymond McGrath. The building's Portland stone façade is supported by steel and features the sculpture 'Prospero and Ariel', by artist Eric Gill.

Renaissance Revival

The word 'renaissance' can be translated as rebirth and as such 'renaissance revival' is an oxymoron. Renaissance architecture flourished in the 14th to 16th centuries, taking influence from ancient Greek and Roman design. The Renaissance Revival style could in itself be split into numerous different schools, such is its diversity. The term was used throughout much of the 19th and into the early 20th century to describe buildings built in broadly classical styles that adhered to ideals of proportion and symmetry laid down in the 15th century but didn't adhere strictly to one tenet, such as Greek Revival, for example. Instead, architects from different countries were influenced by the stylistic quirks of the day – Italianate, Jacobean and Gothic traits, for example – and so included them in their designs.

Modern Classic

Located on Fifth Avenue, New York, the Flatiron Building (1902) is a steel-framed structure with a classical façade. The three-sided building's most acute corner is curved like a giant column and the façade itself is broken into three – base, midsection and top – like the base, shaft and capital of a Greek column.

Style Combinations (right)

At Salle Favart (1889), Paris, France, the combination of Greek and Roman styles can be appreciated, in the many statues and round-topped arches, respectively. Classical columns and rusticated stonework also add to the renaissance mix of the opera house.

Colonial signature (left)

This covered arcade, running along the lower level of the Army Navy Building (1847) in Mumbai, India, is just one element of this building that serves to remind passers-by of the colonial past and western influences that the country experienced.

Pediments and pilasters (right)

St Paul's Basilica (1889), in Toronto, Canada, shows how decoration was an important part of the Renaissance Revival style. The simple structure of the church is adorned with pilasters (decorative columns) and a pediment (the ornately framed triangular roof gable).

Renaissance Revival

Crowning cupola

The huge clock tower, or cupola, that crowns Stockport Town Hall (1908), England, is a dominant feature in this classically inspired building. Its design includes Greek columns and numerous pediments – arches above the clock faces, and triangular pediments higher still. Both types are termed 'broken' because their horizontal portions are incomplete.

Termed 'modern' in this book because of its influence at the start of the 20th century, Renaissance Revival architecture was almost the last hurrah for those who favour classically inspired design. However, the genre's importance cannot be understated due to its foundations in scale and proportion, and the use of elements such as the Roman arch.

The design of the Stockport Town Hall (below) incorporates numerous styles and has a fine symmetry of design as well as a wonderful use of classical Greek columns with scrolled, Ionic capitals. The windows also indicate diverse influences – Roman arches to the lower floor, flatter segmental arches above and Georgianesque flat-headed windows to the upper floor.

Many motifs

The Buenos Aires House of Culture (1898)
is a fine example of decorative Renaissance
architecture, with pediments, pilasters,
friezes above windows, classical balustrades
to the balconies, stone urns and even a
crowning cupola.

Interior glamour

The Moscow Metro, in Russia, has been
built in many architectural styles. The
station at Komsomolskaya (1952) takes
on a Renaissance theme. Note the contrast
between the modern train and the
wonderful decoration of the station's ceiling.

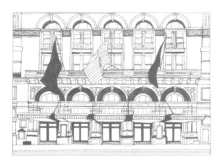

Symmetrical ideals

The front façade of Carnegie Hall, (1891),
in Buffalo, United States, is a study in
symmetry. While styles such as Victorian
and Gothic architecture often included
designs that were non-symmetrical,
Renaissance Revival architects preferred
the regimented ideals of the ancient
architectural orders.

Shaped gables

These beautiful decorative gables in
Brussels, Belgium, date to around 1890.
Although they are entirely different
in character both are influenced by
Renaissance architecture. Note the
scrolled details, the decorative pilasters
and the crowning pediments.

Beaux Arts

Shining example
Palais Garnier (1861–75), in Paris, France, exemplifies the Beaux Arts style with its rich decoration and styling. Every storey incorporates intricate details, from the statues at the base to Corinthian columns above, arched pediments and the gold cornice around the domed roof.

Similar in style to Renaissance Revival, in its echoing of Roman and Greek sculptural and construction philosophies, Beaux Arts architecture evolved out of France, rather than throughout Europe. It exerted a great influence in France and subsequently in the United States. The style has been taught at the Ecole des Beaux Arts in Paris since 1795 and it became prominent in North America between 1880 and 1920.

While Renaissance designs have a formality to them, Beaux Arts buildings tend more towards the artistic, often with expressive flourishes in their decoration. This trait is similar to the Rococo and Baroque ideals born in France and Italy in the late 18th century. Look out for sculptures and statues in natural poses, often reclined; somewhat oversized balcony detailing; lots of rustication; and liberal use of columns and pilasters.

Domes

Domes often crowned Beaux Arts buildings and here, at the Lady Lever Art Gallery (1922), in Liverpool, England, the dome features wonderfully intricate glass panels that allow light to flood into the building. Note that the heavy supporting structure is ribbed to emphasise its strength.

Roman influenced decor

Roman goddesses Diana and Pomona (left) were favourites with Beaux Arts sculptors. Here, they recline quite naturally, a trait that artists brought from the Rococo style to Beaux Arts architecture.

Classical columns

San Francisco War Memorial Opera House (1927–32), in the United States, is understated in comparison to some Beaux Arts buildings. However, the rusticated first storey and pairs of Doric columns with fluted shafts are indicative of the style.

Rustication

A common decorative element, rustication is used in various different architectural genres. Originally a product of unfinished structural stonework, it became decorative: architects emphasised building elements with square block masonry and wide, open mortar joints.

Beaux Arts

The United States became the centre of the Beaux Arts scene in the late 19th and early 20th centuries, even while the pivotal seat of learning for the style remained in Paris, France. Architects such as Richard Morris Hunt, Henry Hobson Richardson and the master-planner of numerous US cities Daniel Burnham attended the École des Beaux Arts and then took their knowledge back to the United States. There they combined the opulence of the style with new construction techniques such as steel frame to create modern buildings with classically inspired façades, including San Francisco City Hall and New York City's Grand Central Station.

Beaux Arts was the last gasp for classical architecture and its influence waned following the First World War, but the buildings still remain, giving us an insight into a pivotal turning point in global architectural history.

North American legacy

Sun Tower (1911–12), in Vancouver, Canada, was designed by William Tuff Whiteway. Its green-painted dome crowns a hexagonal tower, while nine caryatids (sculpted ladies) support the cornice of the main eight-storey building. The building is clad in terracotta tiles and rusticated brickwork.

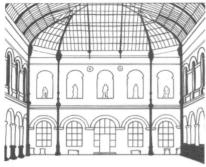

Interior splendour (left)

An interior courtyard at the École des Beaux Arts ('School of Fine Arts'; 1830) in Paris. The space is defined by the partially domed glass roof and slender, wrought-iron pillars. Roman arches, columns, pilasters and sculptures set the Beaux Arts architectural tone.

Palatial Portico (right)

The portico adorning the front of this house is typical of North American domestic Beaux Arts design. Pairs of large columns with scrolled Ionic capitals support a classic triangular pediment, as well as beneath the balcony to complete the grand architectural gesture.

Classical proportion (left)

The Iowa (1900), a famous Beaux Arts apartment building in Washington, D.C., exemplifies the sense of proportion and especially the symmetry instilled into the genre by hundreds of years of classical architectural thinking.

Arts and Crafts

William Morris's home
The Red House (1859–60), in Bexleyheath, England, was designed for Arts and Crafts pioneer William Morris by his friend, architect Philip Webb. The building eschews the high architectural grandeur of the day and instead uses modest materials and an asymmetrical design to express Morris's Arts and Crafts ideals.

Arts and Crafts architecture, which drew inspiration from artisans and craftspeople who worked with their hands, was pioneered by artist and writer William Morris in the United Kingdom, rising to prominence in the 1880s. Morris and his contemporaries rallied against the Industrial Revolution, creating art and architecture that promoted rural and historic trades and crafts. Morris trained as an architect and learned many traditional skills including stonemasonry, wood-carving and metalwork in order to understand better the materials and techniques he aspired to use. The Arts and Crafts movement was taken up by many others and soon the UK had more than 130 associations and organisations devoted to preserving and reviving traditional skills, crafts and art techniques.

American take

The Foursquare, an American institution, was born in the Arts and Crafts era. Modest yet comfortable, and built using honest, sturdy materials and techniques, it epitomises the US take on the Arts and Crafts movement.

Natural materials

Arts and Crafts furniture and interiors relied heavily on wood and metal – natural materials shaped by a craftsperson. Designs also accentuated the techniques used to build each piece, thus championing the maker.

Craftsmanship

This reconstruction of the Morris Chair illustrates the beautiful and yet simple use of natural materials. Leather and wood are combined to create a comfortable and hard-wearing piece of furniture that will last a lifetime.

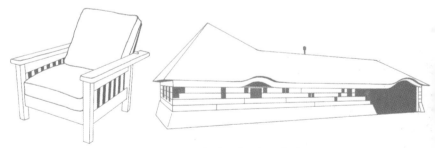

Ancient/modern design

Taking old techniques and making new use of them, this new home, designed by architect David Sellers, is crafted almost entirely from wood. The style, complete with eyebrow eaves detail to the roof, is a take on the Arts and Crafts tradition.

Arts and Crafts

Craftsman house

Built in 1913, by builder Peck McWilliams, this Craftsman house is a Foursquare, influenced by the English Tudor tradition. This English connection can be seen in the use of decorative half timbering on the upper storey and neat square windows with small panes of glass.

In the United States the Arts and Crafts movement took a somewhat different approach to that in the United Kingdom. Often termed American Craftsman style, the US movement's focus centred on creating beautiful homes for the middle classes. Houses with hipped roofs, large, wide verandahs and rustic stone pillars sprang up; bungalows were built with eyebrow dormer windows in gently sloping roofs; and stone homes with Hispanic styling (in the southern states) began to appear with regularity.

American Craftsman style hit the peak of its popularity in the 1930s and such architectural luminaries as Greene and Greene, Bernard Ralph Maybeck and Frank Lloyd Wright followed its tenets. In fact, Lloyd Wright's Prairie Style evolved from the American Craftsman movement. Today, many homes still stand and the style is still practised.

Tell-tale tails (right)

Often, simple elements such as these exposed rafter tails (above the window) were enough to denote that a house was an Arts and Crafts design, the idea being that exposing the timber structure celebrated the craftspeople who constructed the building.

Glass work (left)

Stained glass, a technique developed many years earlier, was a favourite with Arts and Crafts architects in both the United Kingdom and the United States. This American example is indicative of the US style, while British glass tended towards patterns of a more naturalistic type.

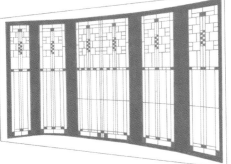

Looking to the past (right)

Taking reference from 14th- and 15th-century Tudor architecture, the Arts and Crafts designers of the 20th century often incorporated large timbers and plaster panels into their work. The trait was so well liked that it is still used today.

23

Art Deco

Egyptian influence

The Carreras Cigarette Factory (1926–28) in Camden Town, London, is a fine example of Art Deco design. Architects Collins, Collins and Porri took an Egyptian theme (inspird by the recent discovery of the tomb of Tutankhamun) and created a colonnade of white columns topped with stylised capitals and a grand entrance guarded by black cats, which were sacred in Egyptian folklore.

The term 'Art Deco' stems from the name of an exhibition of decorative arts that was held in Paris, France in 1925. The architectural style itself is flamboyant and unrestrained, often taking reference from the artistic world, as well as historic antiquity.

However, take a closer look at an Art Deco building and you will recognise architectural standards passed down from classical Roman and Greek design. Proportion, symmetry and scale all play particularly important roles in Art Deco designs, and architects were quick to use classically inspired columns, pediments and arches as backdrops on which to design showpiece industrial and commercial buildings, retail outlets and hotels.

Decorative Art (left)

This mosaic on the façade of a multi-residence building in Paris is an early example of Art Deco artistry being used in architecture. It is more subtle than the Egyptian-inspired designs, and tends towards a more naturalistic feel than the later angled designs seen often in the United States.

Curvaceous designs (right)

The Clifton Hill apartment building, in Melbourne, Australia (1937–38) is shaped to mimic the bridge of an ocean-going liner, the most glamorous method of travel in the 1930s. Sweeping curves, symmetry and glazed tiles (on the central decorative panel) create a landmark Art Deco building.

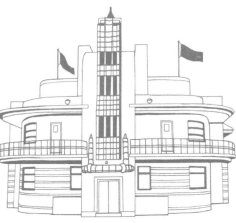

Cuban chic (left)

Havana, Cuba, is the location for this striking Art Deco cinema building. Cine Teatro Fausto (1938). Note how the façade design is unusually not symmetrical. The horizontal ribs and vertical midsection to the façade create a decorative design without the need for further embellishment.

Art Deco

San Fran cool
Originally called the
Pacific Bell Building,
140 Montgomery, in San
Francisco is a 26-storey
Art Deco tower designed
by Miller & Pfleuger in
1924. The building's
stone façade is crowned
by eight giant stylised
eagles, two looking out
from each side of the
square tower.

Art Deco design influenced the architectural scenes in
Europe and the United States in different ways. While
in the United Kingdom and France it was taken to
heart by the designers of mid-size city buildings and
even single homes, in the US the style was championed
by the architects of some of what were then the tallest
buildings in the world.

Many cities across the United States and Latin
America have a clutch of towers that stand out
from their newer Modernist neighbours due to their
extravagant styling – green copper crowns and
gargoyles. These behemoths grew like giant stacked
wedding cakes, their corners and tips
adorned with stylised Greek gods or
Egyptian pharaohs. Art Deco architecture in
American cities is a glorious reminder of a
glamorous past that was all but snuffed out
by the Great Depression
of the 1930s and the
Second World War.

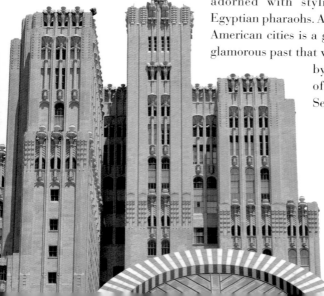

Crowning glory (right)

In New York, the American Standard Building (1924), otherwise known as the American Radiator Building, stands 103 m (340 ft) tall. Its crown takes inspiration from Gothic designs with many pinnacles and turrets, finished in gold to contrast the black brick of the façade.

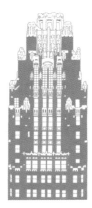

Getting a handle on it (right)

Even something as simple as a door handle can denote an architectural style. Here, the vertical fan style ribs of this handle plate, along with the subtle curved detail on the handle itself are indicative of the Art Deco era.

Colourful ideals (left)

Set on a white backdrop, a plethora of colours comes together in the facade of the Berkeley Shore Hotel (1940). This candy colouration was a favourite for Art Deco designers working on hotels in Miami, Florida.

Interior glamour (right)

Interior design matched the flamboyance of building exteriors and here at the Chatwal Hotel (1905), in New York, the lobby bars and public spaces exude Art Deco cool. Elegant wood panelling, geometric designs on the floors and vertical strip lighting trimmed with shiny steel create a glamour not since matched.

Art Nouveau

Art Nouveau ('New Art') became popular as an art form in the latter part of the 19th century. Reacting against an art and design world dominated by historicism and elitism, practitioners of Art Nouveau encouraged everyone to consider art and design as a part of everyday life. The philosophy spread quickly throughout Europe and as far afield as Australia. Different countries gave the genre local names such as 'Stile Liberty' in Italy and 'Tiffany Style' in the United States.

Architects were quick to catch on to this new, all-embracing art form and adopted a style full of organic lines, picturesque statements and natural motifs such as leaves and vines. They applied them to everything, from stair balustrades and window surrounds to entire building façades, taking architecture in a vibrant and exciting new direction, free from the rigours of a history dominated by symmetry and uniformity.

Belgian bravado
Built in 1905 by Paul Cauchie, Maison Cauchie in Brussels, Belgium illustrates the stepping-stone from historic architectural ideals to Art Nouveau. See the circular window and also the dramatic paintings on the façade – very unusual additions for their time.

Sculpting everywhere

The more flamboyant the better in the Art Nouveau world: this doorway is draped in organic carvings, elevating the mundane to a whole new level. The door itself features unusual surrounds and curved ironwork to complement the stonework above.

Colourful creations

Rather than stick with one material colour, Art Nouveau architects and artists learned how to enliven their designs with different hues. The pilasters and sweeping curves of the arch on this Russian house are accentuated with clever and artistic use of subtle colours.

Arches and curves

The ornate ironwork at the head of two columns at the Grand Palais in Paris (1900) features a multitude of curves, rolls and scrolls and, in the centre, the almost elliptical frame for a cartouche; everything is painted in gold.

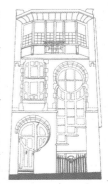

Asymmetry accentuated

How to turn a doorway into a work of art: bursting with Art Nouveau flair, this doorway exemplifies the genre's love of asymmetric designs and artistic flourish. Note the decorative ironwork on the door and the beautifully curved stonework arch.

Art Nouveau

Gaudí's unfinished masterpiece

The Sagrada Familia (begun 1882) is a Roman Catholic church in the centre of Barcelona, Spain. Designed by Antoni Gaudí, it evokes the spires and pinnacles of Gothic religious architecture but subverts them with myriad Art Nouveau flourishes. It has a completion date of 2028, more than 140 years after it was started.

Perhaps no city is so famous for its Art Nouveau architecture and for a single man's work as Barcelona – home to Antoni Gaudí. Ranging from apartment buildings to a park and the astounding, and as yet, unfinished Sagrada Familia Cathedral, Gaudí's designs are a remarkable coming together of art and architecture.

True to the ideals of the Art Nouveau philosophy, Gaudí left no part of his buildings unconsidered with regards to artistic flourish. Entire façades are moulded into curvaceous forms; chimney pots twist as they rise; panels and friezes are adorned with coloured terracotta – the extravagant quirks go on and on.

But while his work is almost ostentatious, Gaudí himself was the opposite. In fact, he died after being hit by a tram and left injured on the roadside because passers-by thought him a beggar.

Inspired by nature (right)

Naturalistic design dominated the Art Nouveau scene and architects/ artists used animal and bird imagery in their work. Here a peacock motif is part of the decorative ironwork for a doorway that includes scrolled grills and leaf-like plates.

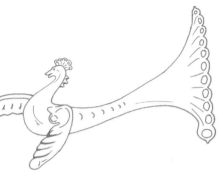

Interior flourishes (left)

The interior of buildings were not neglected, either. Here, a spiral staircase at Paris's Musée Gustave Moreau (1878) illustrates the beauty of Art Nouveau curves and ornate scrolled ironwork achieved by designers and builders of the day.

Curved glass (right)

Taking the ordinary to the next artistic level is what Art Nouveau was all about and how better to elevate a window than dress it in an ornate curved frame and also curve the very glass within it.

Early Modernism

The Isokon Building (1934), designed by Wells Coates, was the first of many deck-access housing blocks in the United Kingdom. Its plain white exterior, punched-out window openings and external walkways are a marked contrast to Art Deco buildings of the same era.

Even as the hedonistic designs of Art Nouveau and Art Deco flourished there was an undercurrent of discontent within the architectural world. A new breed of architect was emerging: one who looked for inspiration not to the art world, but to the function of the buildings themselves. Modernism in the form that we most often perceive it was on the verge of being born.

Led by European practitioners and the Bauhaus school in Germany, functionalist architects eschewed decoration and instead concentrated on designing buildings that would perform best for those who used them. Steel, reinforced concrete and flat plate glass were the materials in favour: roofs lost their pitches, becoming flat because designs dictated large internal spaces, their roofs supported on grids of columns. The form of the building followed its function, a phrase that was often uttered by early Modernist architects.

A new ideal (right)

Now a US landmark, Gropius House (1938), Lincoln, Massachusetts, designed by Walter Gropius, is the epitome of Early Modernist residential design – flat roof, strip window, white painted walls. Contrast this with Max Gate, the Victorian home of Thomas Hardy, and the paradigm shift from ornate to functional becomes entirely apparent.

New materials (left)

Long Beach Airport Terminal (1923), United States, hints at the Art Deco era – its ocean liner aesthetic apparent – but the lack of artistic flourish and minimal metal window frames give away the architect's leanings when it came to design philosophy.

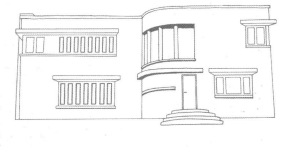

LONG BEACH AIRPORT

New form (right)

Until now pitched roofs had always been the norm, even on large buildings such as factories. But with Early Modernism came the flat roof. Modernist homes almost always sported one and the flat roof became a signature for the Modernist architect. Even today, architects often tend towards them in designs for bespoke homes.

Early Modernism

An American dream
Frank Lloyd Wright's
Robie House (1910) in
Chicago has cantilevered
roof eaves that cover
outdoor living spaces
and bands of windows
that allow light to flood
inside. Dubbed Prairie
Style, due to the flat, low
and expansive design,
the house would become
an icon, only surpassed
by the architect's later
residence, Fallingwater
built in 1935.

While Walter Gropius led the Bauhaus school in Europe, in the United States architects such as Frank Lloyd Wright and Louis Sullivan began to make their mark, too. Using new materials while integrating existing ideals into a new style of architecture, they brought the United States into the Modernist architectural age.

Sullivan was renowned for his office buildings. Always robust and boxlike (with no tiered façades), they were built with new methods and materials but often included classic styling such as arches or scrolled motifs. Lloyd Wright took on the residential sector with his Prairie Style house; its low-slung roofs and expansive footprint becoming a hallmark not just of his work but of almost all US homes for many years to come.

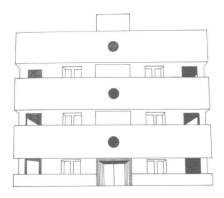

Bare essentials (left)

Israel is not the first place you might look for Early Modernist buildings but architect Ben-Ami Shulman designed numerous buildings in Tel Aviv, including 34 Nachmani Street (1935). Shulman's designs stripped away all non-essential elements to create a minimal style that came to be commonplace in Europe.

Rationalising design (right)

The Casa del Fascio (1936), in Como, Italy is a perfect example of architectural design being refined to perfection. The concrete frame is visible and partially shades the set-back windows; vertical circulation is in the solid right-hand end of the building; no decorative elements are added.

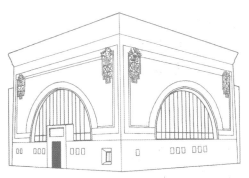

Combining old and new (left)

National Farmer's Bank (1908) in Owatonna, Minnesota, was designed by Louis Sullivan. The brick building is a square box, sturdy and utilitarian in form, as a Modernist bank should be. But Sullivan couldn't resist a little decoration, which harks back to his classical training.

International

International house

Villa Tugendhat (1928–30), in Brno (Czech Republic), was designed by Ludwig Mies van der Rohe. It is built using reinforced concrete and features the balconies and terraces indicative of Internationalism, as are the white painted exterior and metal, rectangular windows.

The International movement was born in the United States in the late 1920s and early 30s. While embracing trendy materials of the time – concrete, steel and glass – its proponents sought to propel the style to the forefront of design by making grand statements such as cantilevered structures and almost transparent buildings.

Characteristics to look out for in International Style buildings are rectilinear forms, a complete lack of ornamentation, empty central courtyards, slender columns (piloti) and the aforementioned cantilevers.

Many architects practised this style and it proliferated following the Second World War due to the ease with which large urban developments could be designed. The rationalisation of construction materials and methods made for swift building and the style represented a crisp, clean new beginning for many cities following the horrors of the war.

Window dressing

Rectangular windows, often linked as a long strip, running flat within the façade, are a hallmark of the International school of design and a mainstay of Modernist architecture. The frames are almost always metal and unless updated, the glass is single-glazed.

Façade without frills

The Turun Sanomat office building (1928–30) in Turku, Finland, was designed by Alvar Aalto. Its façade is completely devoid of decoration, save for the windows, a sure sign that the architect was adhering to the stripped-down International approach.

Machine, for living

Like a bungalow, with all living space on one floor, Le Corbusier's Villa Savoye (1928–31) near Paris, France, rationalises home life. Large relaxation spaces – a living room and a terrace – give way to a smaller kitchen, bedrooms and bathrooms that are tucked together in a cluster.

Machine, for working

Bauhaus founder Walter Gropius designed the Fagus Works (1911–13) in Germany. The factory eschewed the fancy corbelled brickwork of its Victorian predecessors, opting for minimal decoration (lines of brick above the entrance), large window openings and a general feel of functionality.

International

Functional art

The Neue Nationalgalerie (1968) in Berlin was designed by Ludwig Mies van der Rohe. Its upper storey has a prestressed steel roof supported on just eight columns. All the walls are glass. The main exhibition spaces are below, in the lower storey.

The International Style was the antithesis of almost every architectural genre before it. Practitioners disdained the decoration of buildings for purely aesthetics and took the ideas of form following function, first mooted by early Modernists, to their most extreme. This stripped-down design suited austere times, both in terms of the style and message that buildings promoted and also the need to construct commercial and industrial buildings quickly and cost effectively.

Stone and masonry, the two stalwarts of the Industrial Revolution, were pushed aside as architects designed buildings supported by reinforced concrete and shrouded in glass. The ideals of Gropius and Lloyd Wright now had new champions in Ludwig Mies van der Rohe, Le Corbusier and Philip Johnson.

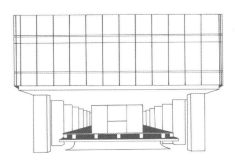

Pillars and posts (left)

An office tower that floats above the ground, supported only on a series of concrete columns, with the public free to walk right underneath … What once would have seemed preposterous now became common, with the use of reinforced concrete and International/ideals.

Rectilinear form (right)

Homes changed forever as the Modernists swept through. Gone were pitched roofs and bay windows, replaced by flat roofs and while walls. Windows were either punched through the wall or became walls themselves, but either way everything had a rectangular feel to it, a rigid aesthetic that ruled for many years.

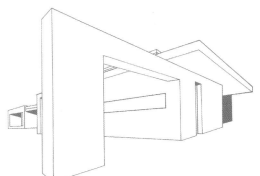

Glass glass glass (left)

A slab of a skyscraper, the United Nations Secretariat Building (1952) in New York has concrete bookends while its two large façades are clad entirely in glass. The building was designed by Le Corbusier and Brazilian Oscar Niemeyer. It is 154 m (505 ft) tall.

Modernism

An architect's home

Architect Erno Goldfinger designed 1–3 Willow Road (1939) in Hampstead, London, England: the largest, central home in the terrace of three houses was for his own family. The building is reinforced concrete with a brick façade. Note the large band of windows and the concrete piloti.

As we have already seen, modern architecture encompasses much more than first imagined, from Beaux Arts to Brutalism and beyond. Modernism is a style within this gamut and one that still holds much influence today.

Born in the early years of the 20th century, Modernism was first championed by the architects we mentioned in Early Modernism (page 34); what followed, in the period between the world wars and beyond, was an evolution of that style.

Modernist architects of the 1930s, 1940s and 1950s took the mantra 'form follows function' and ran with it, making it their own. Le Corbusier developed his 'machine for living' in Villa Savoye, one of the most famous Modernist houses ever – and his peers around the world designed a new style of house, apartment and workplace, which they saw as being better aligned with the social and technological changes of the time.

Expressing ideas (left)

Einstein Tower (1921), in Potsdam, Germany was designed by Expressionist architect Erich Mendelsohn. Its form is in part due to its function as an observatory but Mendelsohn had fun with the design, creating fluid curves and organic shapes more akin to Art Nouveau than Modernism, hence the building's Expressionist tag.

Minimising matters (below)

Minimalism is perhaps the strictest of Modernist philosophies. Architects practising it strip away all unnecessary paraphernalia and design with the intent of creating the perfect building or space. Here, John Pawson's Moritzkirche, in Germany, is a reworking of a 1000 year old church. Pawson has created a pristine white space, devoid of distraction for worshipers.

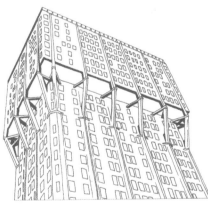

Brutal ideals (above)

Modernism itself also encompassed various subgenres including Brutalism, a term used to describe buildings in which concrete is the predominant material, both structurally and aesthetically. The term comes from French *béton brut* ('raw concrete') and is apt when describing buildings such as Torre Velasca (1958) in Milan, Italy.

Modernism

Modernist art

The Guggenheim Museum (1959), in New York, is Frank Lloyd Wright's most famous building. It is an astounding example of how architectural form can be elevated to create a truly beautiful ideal. There is no decoration, no unrequired elements; simply the external expression of the spiral ramp within.

As the Modernist era advanced, architects strove to create buildings that not only functioned perfectly but also looked great – they took note of the Art Nouveau philosophy and elevated their designs to create art forms out of such aspects as window openings, the interplay between external surfaces and the patina of the materials themselves.

The goal of the Modernist architect of the 1950s and 1960s was to design a building whose functions were clearly defined, while simultaneously presenting a form and material palette that showcased that design to the best effect. As such, structural elements were often exposed both internally and on the exterior; lines were bold and straight; and the interior spaces tended to be open-plan, rather than cellular.

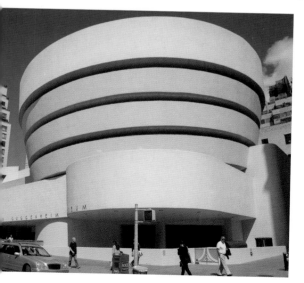

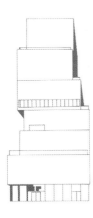

Boxes galore

The New Museum of Contemporary Art (2007), also in New York City, evokes a stack of boxes. The architects, Japanese firm SANAA, designed a series of galleries set above one another and sought to express that in the building's form.

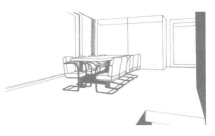

Uncluttered interiors

What does a dining room require other than a dining table? This interior design strips the space of anything that is not vital to the dining experience and as such concentrates the visitor's mind, and heightens expectations of the meal to come.

See-through design

Large-pane glazing was a revelation for the International school of architects and ever since then Modernists have been using it due to its almost invisible appeal. Total-wall glazing lets in lots of natural light and also presents the kind of clean, smooth surface to which Modernist architects are often drawn.

Learning new tricks

The cantilever came of age with the invention of reinforced concrete. Until then, a balcony could project only as far as a brick or stone corbel, or as far as a wooden brace could support. Modernist architects leapt at the chance to cantilever buildings out over thin air. This new house, named Balancing Barn (2010), is by Dutch firm MVRDV.

Postmodernism

Postfunctional
Looking like the bridge of a giant ocean-going liner, the Secret Intelligence Services (SIS) Building (1994) in London is a perfect example of architecture moving away from the pure functionalism of the Modernist approach. Designed by Terry Farrell, the block has the symmetry and pomp of a classical structure but also the scale and excitement of an Art Deco building.

By the 1970s the relatively strict dictats of Modernism were beginning to wear thin for many, and the movement's shortcomings had begun to be fully understood. New buildings began to spring up that had something different about them – a new swagger, even a playfulness of design that had not been seen since the elegance of the Art Deco period: Postmodernism was born.

Postmodern architects wanted to bring back colour and decoration into the architectural world, to counteract the blandness of Modernism. Building designs once again took reference from ancient Roman and Greek architecture, but also drew inspiration from the wider culture and the art world, where the Russian Expressionists and abstract art were all the rage.

Postmodernism (right)

Der Neue Zollhof (1998), by Frank Gehry, is a mixed-use development on the harbour in Düsseldorf. The buildings are typical of Gehry's playful approach to architecture, their forms twisting and undulating to contrast the more typical straight up and down of architecture.

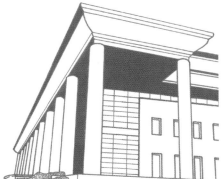

Adding ornament (left)

Taking classical ideals and adding them to a contemporary building can work, sometimes. Here, an office building in Ontario, Canada, has a stylised colonnade with metal columns that border a glass-walled entrance lobby.

Ancient origins (right)

The Piazza d'Italia (1978) in New Orleans, United States, is a cartoonish Postdepiction of an ancient Roman square. All kinds of classical architectural elements are bunched together and painted in many colours. This is an example of why Postmodernism was a short-lived genre.

Postmodernism

Iconic irony?

The Cathedral of Our Lady of the Angels (2002), in Los Angeles, United States, is an iconic landmark. Designed by Rafael Moneo, the huge church is the third largest in the world and its main doors weigh 25 tonnes. Above them is a contemporary statue of the Virgin Mary, while the building itself is a concrete edifice adorned with religious iconography.

Even architects indelibly linked with the Modernist movement grew tired of its rigours and displayed their discontent in new buildings that almost made a mockery of Modernism's 'form follows function' idealism. Famously, Philip Johnson, the architect who coined the name 'International Style', designed the AT&T Building (1981–84; now the Sony Building) in New York City, its Modernist façade topped with an open pediment, while at its base stands a huge Roman arch.

Such statements became the trademark of the Postmodernist architect, and for a while the style prevailed, but, without serious ideals, Postmodernism slowly dissolved into the background in the late 1990s as the majority of architects remained faithful to their Modernist education.

Having fun with design (left)

Islington Square (2006) in New Islington, Manchester, England, is a housing development by architect FAT. Built in brick but entirely different from the norm, FAT's design transforms the streetscape with a series of facades that ape the Beaux Arts buildings of the Netherlands, and which are shot through with different-coloured brickwork.

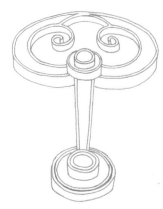

Symbolism (right)

Taipei 101 (1999–2003) in Taiwan, for a time the tallest building in the world, is adorned with a contemporary take on the Ruyi, an ancient ceremonial symbol used in Chinese Buddhism. The symbol on the tower is definitely modern but it is used as in ancient times to symbolise protection and healing for those within.

Mocking architecture (left)

Some buildings cannot really be classified as architecture. However, if buildings such as this giant bird garage in the United States were to be lumped into a genre then it would have to be Postmodern, simply because of their anti-architectural ideals.

Avant Garde

New civic ideas

The SBS TV headquarters (1997–2002) in Federation Square, Melbourne, Australia, is shrouded in a façade of tessellated triangles. It is one of a number of bizarre buildings in the square, which was initially hated by the general public. The square, designed by LAB Architecture Studio, has since been recognised as an architectural triumph.

The Avant Garde school of architecture is a difficult one to categorise, simply because 'avant garde', meaning vanguard or advance guard, is used to describe artists, architects and other creatives who are at the forefront of their art, those who are experimenting and pushing boundaries. All architects who have challenged an accepted genre could be considered Avant Garde.

In this book we shall investigate some architects and buildings from the past and also look at those who are changing the way we think about our built environment now – and there are many of them, as new technologies and materials make what might have seemed impossible just a decade ago the perfect answer to a design conundrum today.

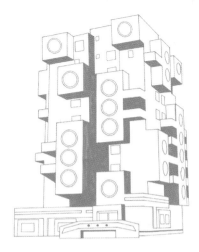

A different perspective

In the 1950s and 60s much was being made of uniformity and mass production, as the Modern era strode forward. However, some architects couldn't resist adding a new dimension to their Modernist buildings. This residential building was built in Babruysk, Belarus.

Changing the norm

Avant Garde does not have to be totally new, unseen before. Here, the Inntel Hotel (2010) in Zaandam, Netherlands, is a wonderful reimagining of the Beaux Arts architecture popular in that country at the start of the 20th century. WAM Architecten took the norm and twisted it to create something new and exciting.

Bending ideas

It could be called Postmodern or Deconstructivist, but the Art Gallery of Alberta in Canada (2010) is definitely doing one thing – and that is pushing the boundaries of architectural design in western Canada. The country is not renowned for its Avant Garde architects and so when Los Angeles architect Randall Stout designed this building it really made waves.

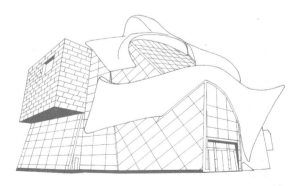

Avant Garde

Avant Garde architects and artists are often derided initially because their work seems so much at odds with what is currently accepted. However, as time and perceptions change, what was once thought of as left field and strange often comes to be seen as the way forward. Architects such as Le Corbusier and Antoni Gaudí forged new beginnings and schools of thought earlier in the century. Today, big names such as Zaha Hadid and Jurgen Mayer build fantastical buildings that change the way we perceive our built environment. It should be acknowledged, though, that these two current architectural stars strove to get their work built for many years without success – so little was their vision in tune with the ideas of policymakers and public ideals at the time.

New forms

Houses are the architecture that we all know best but when presented with one that turns what we know upside down, how do we react? This Japanese house does just that. Its form and bunker-like appearance are off-putting but what lies inside? Our curiosity is aroused, the architect has us thinking and exploring new possibilities.

Material challenges (below)

Taking materials and making them do things differently is pushing boundaries. At the CCTV Building (2004–12) in Beijing, China, architect OMA redefined the structural steel grid, using advanced techniques to calculate loads and shear forces, in order to create the unusual latticework that supports this unique skyscraper.

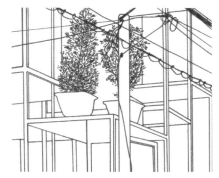

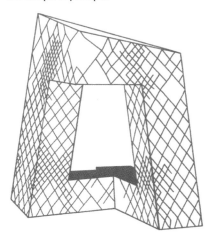

Internal conundrums (above)

What if the exterior of a house is a transparent film, and the interior a series of stepped spaces? Can you live in such a paradox? House NA (2011), by Sou Fujimoto Architects in Tokyo, Japan, is asking those questions. The answers may never be clear but the Avant Garde architect will already have moved on to pose more quandaries.

Shock value (right)

There are not really words to describe the façade of the Scottish Parliament Building (2004) in Edinburgh, Scotland. The building cost millions of pounds more than originally estimated, causing public outcry; but architecturally it was seen as a tour de force that challenged the ideals of High Tech architecture and took decorative architectural design into a new era.

Deconstruction

Battling with the norm
The Imperial War Museum North (2002), in Manchester, England, is designed by an architect considered to be both Avant Garde and Deconstructivist: Daniel Libeskind. His concept tells the story of war as represented by the globe shattered and reassembled; the three fragments – earth, air and water – interlocked to form the museum space.

The Deconstructivist architect throws aside the Modernist ideal that 'form follows function' – just as Postmodernism did. However, Deconstructivism takes the next step and actually attempts to blow apart the common idea of a building by literally deconstructing it (usually its façade) and rebuilding it in a new and often unrecognisable way.

Fragmentation and manipulation of surface and form create a whole new set of challenges for the architect and the users of these buildings. Public perception has always been tricky with such radical redesign of the norm and many Deconstructivist buildings are initially not well received. However, the human mind is ever-curious, and, what might at first look seem jarring, becomes an interesting new ideal when reconsidered: such are the challenges of architectural Deconstructivism.

Disassembled station (left)

This mêlée of tilted posts and slanting surfaces is the Neue Mitte Oberhausen train station (1996) in Germany. The design looks as if an ordered platform has been taken apart and then thrown back together in a giant heap – the complete deconstruction of what we consider a local commuter railway station to be.

Fragmented art (right)

A series of rectangular boxes, stacked, jutting out, and then a darker cuboid emerging from within; this building is instantly interesting to every passer-by. The Contemporary Arts Center (2001–03), Cincinnatti, United States, was designed by Zaha Hadid and its fragmented form made it universally recognised. While sticking to the Modernist ideal of straight lines, Hadid has subverted the building's form by disconnecting its elements with shifts in form and colour.

Distortion of surface (right)

Daniel Libeskind is a master of deconstructivism and his The Crystal, a new entrance to the Royal Ontario Museum (2007) in Toronto, Canada, creates an addition to a historic building that totally contrasts the existing construction and challenges anyone who dares recognise it to come up with a description worthy of the myriad angles and non-parallel lines that make up the building.

Deconstruction

Crumpled fabric

Frank Gehry's Cleveland Clinic Lou Ruvo Center for Brain Health (2007–09), in Las Vegas, United States, looks as if it's melting. The design crumples the health center's façade in a dramatic statement that twists the building's form into what a few years ago would have been considered impossible shapes.

While Postmodernists often adhered to Modernist ideals with regards to the spatial function of a building, designing it rationally before adding decoration to distance it from the genre, Deconstructivists sought to rally against the core of Modernism and do away with geometry and recognised spatial thinking.

In order to achieve this new idealism, Deconstructivist architects have often taken recognised building forms and subverted them, giving the viewer a glimpse of what should be, before radically altering it. Gehry did this with his own home in Santa Monica (Gehry Residence, 1978), and the UFA Kristallpalast (1997–98) in Dresden by Coop Himmelb(l)au tilts a glass tower on its side, changing the way we view what has become standard.

Non-conforming design (right)
Daniel Libeskind's first widely recognised building, the Jewish Museum (2001) in Berlin, Germany, is designed around the concept of an abstracted Star of David, and the connecting of lines that link locations of historical events, so informing the zigzag plan view of the building.

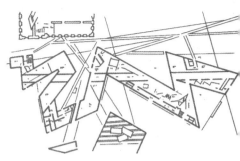

Adding deconstruction (left)
A classical building in a formal neighbourhood in Dresden, Germany; but what this architect has done with the fire escape (2006) is amazing, taking a mundane but regulatory necessary addition and turning it into a showstopper with a little Deconstructivist magic.

Partial alien (right)
On a classically designed apartment building in Falkstrasse, in Vienna, Austria, architect Delugan Meissl has added a penthouse apartment (2010) – but classical it is not. Like a crashed alien spaceship, the form and façade of the apartment are a jumble of twisted metal and pointed shards; the result, a jarring contrast to the building below.

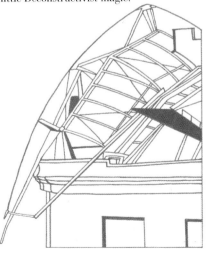

Fusion

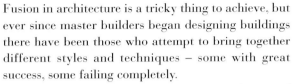

Design with nature
Namba Parks (2003–07) is a commercial and retail development in Osaka, Japan. Designed on a sloping site, the curving outdoor malls are heavily landscaped with trees to bring nature into the heart of one of the country's busiest cities.

Fusion in architecture is a tricky thing to achieve, but ever since master builders began designing buildings there have been those who attempt to bring together different styles and techniques – some with great success, some failing completely.

Architects have many styles, philosophies and geographic trends to choose from when designing. Even before our technological age, in which architects can easily check out ideas and builds from anywhere on the planet, the design world was rife with practitioners sharing their work. Ever since the Renaissance period in the 15th century, architects have been fusing new ideas with ancient edicts on scale and proportion: French and English Renaissance architects incorporated their national ideas into teaching coming out of Italy. Today, there are so many styles and subgenres that architects have a hard time designing to a single philosophy; many slip easily between styles to create buildings that are considered a fusion of multiple genres.

Ancient influence

The entrance to this modern office block in Perth, Australia, takes the form of a stylised ancient portico. The line of columns features composite capitals (from Roman times) but with smooth shafts and unornamented bases, which could be Doric. The portico makes for a dramatic contrast to the Modernist building behind.

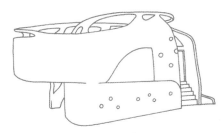

Organic form

Ushida Findlay Architects was itself a fusion of Japanese and Scottish architects, Eisaku Ushida and Kathryn Findlay. Together the duo designed buildings including this, the Truss Wall House in Tokyo (1993), which fused Modernist ideals with the most fluid of organic forms.

Victorian-Modernist combination

In Creemore, Canada, this Victorian-style farmhouse with a steeply pitched roof is perfectly complemented by a modernist addition, added in 2011 similar materials are used to blend the two contrasting styles and make for thought-provoking architecture.

Classical Modern

This Romanian office building is located in an historic house of the Beaux Arts period. However, the addition above is most definitely in the contemporary Modern style. The two elements contrast in such a way that each highlights the other without overshadowing it.

Fusion

Much fusion architecture comes from the need to add to existing buildings. When such a situation arises the architect can either attempt to design in the same style as the original building or bring new aesthetics and architectural ideas to bear on the project. Either option is tricky: with the first, the need to match faithfully with often historic architecture using modern materials is challenging; with the latter comes the need to be sensitive to the existing building while differentiating the new from it in such a way that both elements are presented in their best light.

When an architect chooses to fuse styles in a brand-new building there are thus significant challenges. Styles, eras and genres have been born out of a need to break free from the old and create a new way; combining such defining architectural principles can be a risky business.

Old base, new tower
The six-storey base of the Hearst Tower (1928; 2006) in New York City was designed by Architect Joseph Urban in 1928 with the intention for a tower of the same style on top, but it was not until Norman Foster added the High Tech glass and steel tower in 2006 that it was finally completed.

Islam and India

Jama Masjid (1644–56) is the principal mosque of Old Delhi, India. While predominantly Islamic in appearance and design, the mosque is unusual in that it incorporates pointed arches that are traditionally Indian, and a colonnade with 260 pillars all carved in the Hindu and Jain traditions. The two religions and cultures intertwine perfectly in this historic building.

Architecture and art

Charles and Ray Eames were renowned for their clever use of colour in architectural and furniture design. Here, at their own home, Eames House (1949), the couple fused Modernist design with abstract use of colour in the style of Dutch artist Piet Mondrian.

Asian/Modern

US firm Webber Studio designed a home in Texas but instead of seeking to mimic Prairie Style houses the architect took influence from Oriental design – and the results are beautiful. Japanese in flavour, the multipaned glazed wall and minimal arbour/walkway work well with the low-pitched roof of the American Midwest.

Future Modern

Concrete sculpture

Trying to explain the undulating curves of the Pierre Vives Building (2012), in Montpellier, France, is best left to the architect. Zaha Hadid is quoted as describing the inspiration for the public library, archive and sports building as 'the tree of knowledge' conceptualised as an organisational diagram.

Future Modern is a style just waiting to go out of date, purely because of the name. Current architectural trends are pushing in so many different directions that it is difficult to compartmentalise them and, as new techniques and materials are explored, architects are able to create buildings that are ever more unusual and exciting. The term used to describe the current architecture of such design luminaries as Zaha Hadid and Rem Koolhaas, as well as a plethora of new firms that are pushing the boundaries of what can be built, Future Modern is about testing the limits, creating new forms, utilising unusual techniques and designing buildings that react to their surroundings and look like nothing that the world has seen before.

Tomorrow, as we advance yet further, maybe all buildings will be elliptical and have photoreactive skins, then architects will look again to the new, but for now these buildings are our Future Modern.

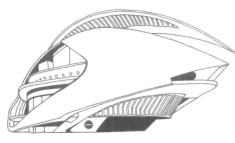

Evolving form (above)

Avant garde, Postmodern, Fusion ... The Palau de les Arts Reina Sofia (2005), in Valencia, Spain, is designed by engineer and architect Santiago Calatrava. Its form defies description and categorisation, but the resulting building is beautiful and spectacular, its stark white exterior reflecting the Spanish sun.

Curvaceous leanings (below)

Who says that skyscrapers have to be straight up and down? The Absolute World Towers (2010–12), in Mississauga, Canada were designed by Chinese firm MAD, and the name is quite apt, as the towers' curvaceous design displays. They have since been dubbed the 'Marilyn Monroe Towers'!

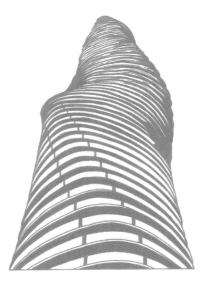

Façades gone mad (left)

Aqua is the name of an 82-storey mixed-use tower (2007–09) in Chicago, United States. The horizontal delineation of the façade undulates in and out of the glass skin, creating contours in the building's surface, which evoke lakes set amidst rolling hills.

Future Modern

Spiky proposition
A pavilion clad in 60,000 optical rods that gently sway in the breeze – this was the United Kingdom Pavilion at the Shanghai Expo 2010. Designed by Thomas Heatherwick, it tests the boundaries of what a building façade is, and, how it might react to outside forces.

Architects have been using computers ever since they became commercially available, but until relatively recently the machines were used purely as tools to calculate and reproduce the 'mechanics' of a building. However, with the advent of creative design software, first two-dimensional and then in 3D, architects tapped into a whole new world of possibilities.

Today, even the simplest of buildings are designed digitally, then reworked and tested for potential failure before they ever get near the construction site. Architects wishing to push boundaries in the design field use technology to help explore possibilities, the extremes of materials and structural form. Buildings are taking on ever more extraordinary shapes and becoming more environmentally friendly. Future Modern buildings are catching up to the sci-fi ideas only seen in films.

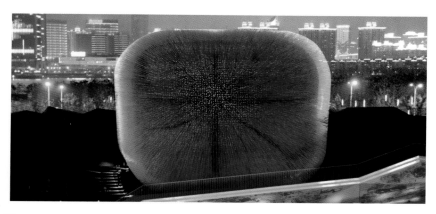

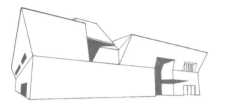

A new Brutalism

Clad in white granite, the Aga Khan Museum (2010–14), in Toronto, Canada, was designed by Fumihiko Maki. The building is austere, almost fortress-like; perhaps a reference to the struggle that Islamic people are going through in the 21st century. The architecture is timeless: Modernism for the future.

Embracing environmentalism

A Modernist at heart, Renzo Piano has created a hybrid building to house the California Academy of Sciences (2008) in San Francisco, United States. The stripped-glass and steel ideals of Modernism are combined with cutting-edge environmental architecture that includes a grass lumpy roof and portholes through it.

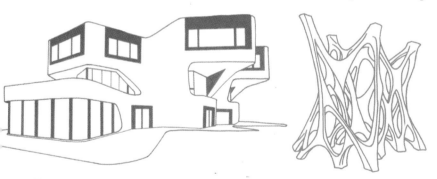

Modernist redux

Modernism morphed into Futurism, maybe. J. Mayer H. Architects' Dupli Casa (2008) is a house in Germany that almost seems poured onto its foundations. With its roots in the Modernism of the 1940s, the house is brought back to the future as Mayer stretches and melds its form to suit the sloping site, and his wild imagination.

Looking to new geometries

Cast Thicket is the winning entry in an architectural competition in which teams used parametric modelling and digital fabrication to design and manufacture new forms with the potential to be used in construction. Designed by Christine Yogiaman and Ken Tracy, the model is now on display in the University of Texas.

Building Types

Equipped with a working knowledge of the major styles of the modern architectural era, we will now investigate the predominant building types to check out how each architectural school of thought affected their design and construction. Beginning with homes, the building type most familiar to everyone, we'll trace the history of each building type's design as materials, technology and architectural philosophy changed and evolved throughout the 20th century and on into the 21st century.

Each chapter will include a section on Archetypes – exemplars of each of the major architectural styles to influence the building type. This collection will illustrate how the building has developed during the last century – and, seen together, will help map out our recent architectural history in an easily decipherable way.

The Featured Buildings pages will then delve deeper into the design and construction of two of the most famous buildings of each type, while in sections entitled Construction and Materials, Doors and Windows, and Ornamentation we'll pick out the elements specific to each architectural genre, and describe why they were influenced by the style, thinking and philosophy of the moment.

This Building Types section of *How To Read Modern Buildings* is your at-a-glance guide to the built environment that surrounds you. Find a building, flick to the section that covers it – Homes, Transport, Religious and so on – and pinpoint the archetype that is most similar to it: simple. Well, maybe not quite that simple – but you'll definitely be set in the right direction to find the styles and ideals that influenced the design of your building.

Introduction

Arts and crafts

W. H. Bidlake built Garth House in Edgbaston, UK in 1901. It is a fine example of the English Arts and Crafts movement. While there is little decoration, much attention was paid to the craftsmanship of windows, doors and surrounds. The asymmetrical design of the building and chimney stacks are also indicative of the genre.

Homes – single-family houses – are the building type with which architects have been given the most design latitude throughout the history of architecture. Domestic buildings of every scale, shape and idiosyncrasy have been built on sites that range from deserts to mountain ranges and even water.

One would think that architects would revel in the freedom that comes with designing a house, but the starting point is often less of a blank sheet of paper than a long list of requirements and constraints set by the client, the environment and the government to ensure that the house in question will stand up to the rigours of everyday living over many years.

Architects have worked hard to adapt and evolve domestic architecture to suit the needs of each generation. As the romanticised ideals of Arts and Crafts homes fell away in favour of a Modernist approach, the house shape and style of living changed. Flat roofs replaced pitched ones, and open-plan spaces superseded cellular rooms. Similarly, the environmental considerations of more recent times have led to changes in building fabric design. Large glazed walls supported by slim steel frames are beginning to

be usurped by highly insulated walls, orientation-specific glazing and alternative means of bringing natural light into the home, such as sun pipes.

The design of the house is shifting and changing almost constantly. However, while evolution and adaptation is ongoing, the guiding principles of what make up a successful home are still apparent, and remain the same as those at the start of the 20th century. Check out any of the genres included in this chapter and you'll see that whether Modernist, Avant Garde, Prairie Style or even Minimal, almost every home is designed around a central living space, with service elements – kitchen, bathrooms and so on – adjoining as satellite units. In some instances, spaces such as the kitchen are integrated into the main space for social interaction but always the area for gathering, bonding and relaxing is principal to the building design. After all, these are the homes in which we live – and as such they need to work well with our dynamic, our family, our life.

Modern

Located in Cape Cod, Massachusetts, the Kugel/Gips House by architect, Charles Zehdner, takes Modernist ideals and turns them into sculpture. Built in 1970, the large house was more recently abandoned for 11 years, until the Cape Cod Modern Trust restored it and it is now available for holiday rental.

Archetypes

Classical beauty
Designed by Richard Morris Hunt, The Breakers (1893) is a grand Renaissance Revival house in Newport, Rhode Island. The building is symmetrical in form and includes decorative features first used centuries ago, in the Renaissance period in France.

While houses have been designed and built in almost every architectural style given a name, some genres have suited the single-family home better than others. Take, for example, the comparison between a Prairie Style bungalow and a Renaissance Revival mansion. While in its truest form, the latter was always the grandest of homes, the Prairie Style bungalow could be designed both big and small with equal success. It became one of the most widely built homes in North America.

That said, we should not dismiss the Renaissance Revival. With this and other grandiose styles there always come a plethora of design nuances that can be transferred to any dwelling. Renaissance architecture championed the ancient rules of symmetry, scale and proportion, all of which should be considered in the design of your standard three-bedroom family home.

Beaux Arts

John Bush House (1903) in Buffalo, United States, has all the attributes of a fine Beaux Arts mansion. More lavishly decorated than a Renaissance house, it has a decorative parapet wall at eaves level while white stone quoins contrast the brickwork at the corners of the building.

Art Deco

Almost Modernist, but not quite: this home's curved front wall and window, together with the balustrade-style railings, add a panache that belies its Art Deco leanings. The use of white painted stucco was common in homes of this type, before being claimed by Modernist architects, too.

Postmodern

With a flat roof but pitched front wall, and with a circular roundel vent, this house is poking fun at its more modest neighbours through the work of a designer who has a flair for almost ironic Postmodern architecture. Note also the quirky balcony railings.

Modernist

Simple and yet exquisitely stylish, this Modernist house is designed as two rectangular volumes stacked. Both spaces face towards the beach – the upper, more private; the lower, allowing views in and out. Their form is defined by the white concrete walls, floor and roof plates, creating a single, unfettered aesthetic.

Archetypes

While each architectural genre has its own set of guiding principles, many designers choose to drift between them when designing homes. This freedom makes for interesting and sometimes rather disturbing results. However, when executed well the combination of styles, even two such opposing ideals as Arts and Crafts and Modernism, can create beautiful homes whose design transcends any style.

This considered, the architect who chooses to mix and match is a brave one. Each genre has its guiding tenets for a reason, and they should not be trifled with lightly. Classical and artistically inspired styles such as Renaissance Revival and Art Nouveau rarely combine well with the more utilitarian design ideals of Brutalism or Deconstructivism. Styles are bound in philosophies for a reason.

Art Nouveau
De Zonnebloem (1900), in Antwerp, Belgium, was designed by Jules Hofman. The curvaceous windows – surrounds and frames – along with dainty floral decoration on the façade and playful balcony tell us that this is an Art Nouveau house. No other genre was so free with its organic expression and artistic intent.

Arts and Crafts

Arts and Crafts homes in the United Kingdom tend towards white walls and red tiled roofs, giving them a staid, homegrown appearance. This grounded aesthetic is tempered by details such as the slight change in pitch of the roof to the left, hinting at a 'saltbox' style house, and the sloping, buttressed wall on the right side.

Fusion

New housing developments often try to differentiate multitudes of similarly designed houses with architectural details. Here, a generic one-and-a-half storey home features an ancient Greek broken pediment above the upper bedroom window and a Georgianesque fanlight above the front door.

Deconstructivism

Daniel Libeskind's prefabricated villa is a lesson in Deconstructivism on a residential scale. The angular forms and protrusions are so alien to the norm that the house ceases to be recognisable as one – and instead becomes a sculptural statement.

Future Modern

Making great use of a tiny site, this Future Modern home design from Japan rethinks the way we live. The bulk of the house cantilevers out over the carport and the living space is set behind a giant window, while the rest of the home is tucked privately behind the blank-faced walls of this geometric oddity.

Materials and Construction

Blanket response

Curtain Wall House (1993–95), in Tokyo, Japan, has a rigid structural steel frame but its walls are billowing fabric curtains. Designed by Shigeru Ban, this bizarre house is an architectural oddity and a lesson that nothing in architecture should be taken for granted.

The materials used to construct houses are, and always have been, many and varied. This is due to the relatively small size of the building, and so the less stressful loading requirements when compared to an industrial building or skyscraper. However, architects in different geographical regions tended towards different materials due to availability and the skill-sets of local craftsfolk. While in the United Kingdom and central Europe stone and masonry were, and still are, the predominant construction materials, in North America, Asia and Australia wood became the most common building material.

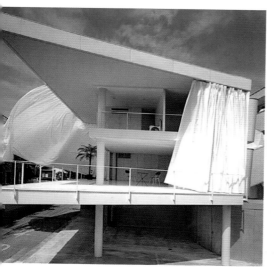

Concrete has been used in construction for thousands of years; however, the means of reinforcing it was developed only in the mid-19th century; the first reinforced concrete bridge was built in 1889. Soon afterwards it began to be used in construction, and the early Modernists saw in it the perfect utilitarian material with which to build their 'machines for living'.

Wooden wonder

The Gamble House (1909), designed by Greene and Greene for David B. Gamble of Procter & Gamble, is an Arts and Crafts home and American treasure. Note the wooden shakes that cover the walls, the ends of the large timber floor beams, and the beautifully crafted entrance door and surround.

Crooked concrete

Poured concrete is cast into moulds called formwork, which are constructed on site in the position that the wall is required. Here, you can see the imprints of the formwork boards left on the concrete external walls of this modern hillside house.

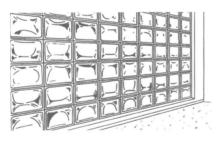

Getting all glassy

Glass is more usually seen in sheets, or panes, but here a wall has been built using glass blocks. As wide as conventional concrete blocks, the square glass blocks are heavy, their glass faces being thick enough to withstand a certain amount of weight in compression, for constructing walls such as this one.

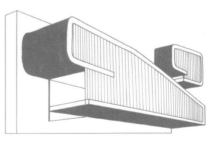

Metal in Madrid

Clip House (2008), by Bernalte-Leon y Asociados, is a Futuristic home of concrete and copper. Supported by the giant concrete spine, the house is clad in sheets of copper, which will slowly patinate and turn green with exposure to the elements.

73

Materials and Construction

With different materials come different construction methods. For many years prior to the modern era house walls were solid – whether built from stone, brick or wood (in the form of logs) – and the thicker the better. However, as technologists began to understand the insulative properties of air gaps, cavities were built into brick walls, while timber-framing became less about huge timbers and more about the structural strength of well-designed 'stick-frame' walls.

While many forms are buildable with wood and stone, steel and concrete (reinforced and prestressed) revolutionised what architects could achieve for relatively low cost. Huge columns could be slimmed down, cantilevers could be made bigger, spans between walls made wider. Early in the 20th century, house design changed, becoming more varied and exciting, and since then architects designing homes have not looked back.

All on show

Modernists believe that the materials used to build the house should be celebrated, not hidden behind decoration; here is a great example of the structural steel beams and columns being highlighted. Picked out in a dark shade, to contrast the white walls and ceiling, the steel creates frames around windows, walls and so on.

One we made earlier

Precast concrete panels were pioneered in Liverpool, England, in the early 20th century. Since then, they have been used to build numerous styles of house including the Airey house, a type of prefabricated home built extensively following the Second World War. The Airey house's precast concrete façade made it quick and cheap to build at a time when there was a shortage of housing.

Green homes

With environmental concerns come new ways of building eco-consciously. This unusual house is built into the hillside, giving it great insulation and protection from the weather, and it has a sedum-planted roof. Solar panels supply electricity, too.

Blurring the lines

In countries with a stable, warm climate architects can design homes with little concern for insulation and climate protection. Instead, walls are removed and living areas merge from interior to exterior seamlessly, the only marker being the change in the floor covering.

Hill House

Scottish gem

Hill House is a grand architectural statement. Vast walls dominate the windows, giving the building a feeling of strength and solidity. Design details such as the setback in the main tower, which reveals the sloping chimney flue, give character, as do the conical roofs to the circular tower and smaller folly below.

Hill House sits high on a hill overlooking the River Clyde, in Helensburgh, Scotland. Designed by Charles Rennie Mackintosh for publisher Walter Blackie and family, the home was completed in 1904.

The architectural design is a mix of styles, from Arts and Crafts to Art Nouveau, Italianate and Japonisme, and as such, could be classed as Fusion. However, Mackintosh was renowned for his Arts and Crafts work and the design is underpinned by this genre.

Blackie agreed to let Mackintosh and his wife Margaret Macdonald design everything about the house inside and out. When Mackintosh had completed his work and handed it over to his client, he is reported to have said to Blackie: 'Here is the house. It is not an Italian Villa, an English Mansion House, a Swiss Chalet, or a Scotch Castle. It is a Dwelling House.'

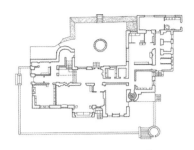

Layout

Mackintosh designed the layout of the house before its structure, planning the main living spaces along one axis and the smaller service areas down another at right angles to it. All living areas – drawing room, dining room and library – look out onto the gardens. Circulation space is pushed to the rear; a very modern aspect of the design.

Asymmetric detailing

Eschewing any notion of symmetry was one of Mackintosh's ways of stamping his mark onto Hill House. This home would not be considered a pastiche of classical architecture, like other grand houses. This façade demonstrates his quirky design attitude perfectly, as not one element is paired with another and yet all fit well on the whole.

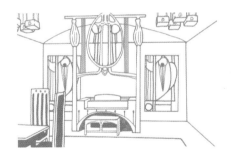

Entrance

The way into Hill House is inconspicuous and a design highlight. While the actual door is of normal proportions and tucked into the side of the entrance lobby, the shape of the space and the tall, thin windows are great clues to Mackintosh's interest in Modernism and the games that could be played with it.

Interior décor

Inside, Mackintosh and his wife let their love of Art Nouveau shine with artistic wall panels and a totally over-the-top surround for the piano in the dining room. Note the high-backed dining chairs; these were a signature design of the architect's.

Doors and windows

Much can be made of the doors and windows in a house, whether through their positioning, size, ornamentation or lack of it. Both have been used as pivotal points in the design of external façades of buildings of all styles in the modern era. The shape of the window or door head is often an at-a-glance guide to the architect's ideals and influences: a semicircular arch is Romanesque and very classical; a pointed arch, Gothic; a fanlight above the door indicates Georgian traits, and so on.

Additionally, the material with which the window frame or door and frame is made, and the style in which it is built, also give significant clues. Sturdy wooden panelled doors with proud wrought iron fittings signal Arts and Crafts intent, while flowing asymmetrical lines and organically inspired curved window openings scream Art Nouveau.

Renaissance Revival

Historic leanings mean that this Renaissance Revival doorway is very formal. Bordered by fluted pilasters and topped with a heavy, decorated transom, the doorway is rooted in ancient architectural idealism. The door itself is split into two slim leafs to add to the formal entrance effect.

Art Nouveau

Wow factor is always a good thing to achieve in architecture but it is often missed. That is not so here, as this Art Nouveau house stands out from its neighbours in part because of the wonderful shape of its windows and balcony surrounds.

Art Deco

Leaded glass – small panes held between a lead framework – was popular at the beginning of the 20th century, and Art Deco designers used the technique to great effect, creating patterned window-panes that matched the stylised architectural flourishes of the buildings in which they were installed.

Beaux Arts

While similar in style to Renaissance, this Beaux Arts doorway takes more liberty with the decorative elements and as such is rather more grand. The pilasters and transom are larger, the doorway itself is arched and carved figures adorn the spandrel, between arch and surround.

Doors and windows

A house for Rose
Australian architect Harry Seidler built Rose Seidler House (1948–50) for his wife. The design exemplifies Modernist tastes of the mid-20th century: white external walls, flat roof, super-thin piloti and an entire wall of windows. This style of home would inspire generations of architects and is still popular today.

As construction technology progressed throughout the 20th century architects began to look at doors and windows in a different light. No longer did they need to be holes punched into the fabric of a solid wall; instead, they could become the wall or be omitted altogether, leaving a void. Advances in prestressed concrete, structural steel beams and other lightweight load-bearing materials meant that the size of the doorway or window could be anything that the architect wanted. This coincided with the rise of Modernism and in particular Internationalism, in which architects vied to create ever more transparent houses. The era of ornamenting the door or window was dead; now it was all about making it disappear in a transparent void.

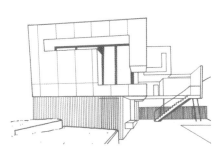

Modern ribbons

This Modernist house, built in 2009 in New York, United States, takes reference from earlier homes of the same style, utilising the thin ribbon window in numerous areas. To the fore, it connects to a glazed door, while in the rear the ribbon is tipped vertically to create interestingly framed views from within and unusual form from the exterior.

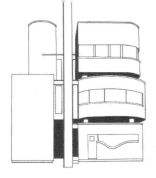

Windows for Wall House

Wall House (2001) by John Hejduk is an unusual Postmodern home in Groningen, the Netherlands. The architect has created three volumes, each differing in form and window shape. The result is a quirky Postmodern design that steers clear of some of the movement's more ironic pastiches of classical architecture.

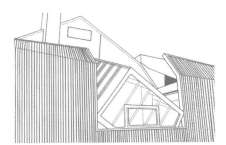

Frank's pad

Frank Gehry House (1978) in Santa Monica, United States, was the architect's home before he became widely known. He practised his craft upon it and created a Deconstructivist design that includes a glazed sunroom that looks as if it has fallen over.

Every which way

Bringing together different styles can work but at times the adage 'less is more' should be adhered to. This house has a bay window on the upper storey, semicircular fanlights and multipane sash windows. The effect is somewhat over the top but all too common in large developer-led housing estates.

Falling Water

Perhaps the United States' most famous architect, Frank Lloyd Wright designed many homes including large mansions and the small Usonian Home for working-class families. However, by far his best-known house is Fallingwater. Built over a waterfall on a creek in Stewart Township, Pennsylvania, the house is a series of cantilevered levels that stretch out above the waterfall, seemingly floating in mid-air.

The house was completed in 1935 and listed as a National Historic Landmark in 1966. Wright's cantilevered design overcame the requirement for a large house on a small site.

In 1991, the American Institute of Architects voted the house, 'best all-time work of architecture' and it is listed in the Smithsonian's Life List of 28 places to visit before you die.

Home over Bear Run

Bear Run, the creek over which Fallingwater sits, flows right underneath the house, which is supported on giant stone walls that can be seen underneath the lowest cantilever. The house itself is grounded by the massive vertical spine wall of stone and the circulation tower joined to it.

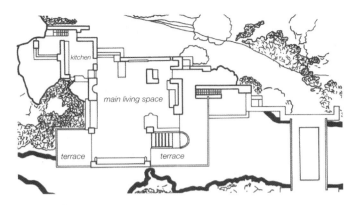

Planning a masterpiece

Frank Lloyd Wright was a Modernist and it shows in his open-plan layout of the main floor of Fallingwater. Dining room, main living space, and two terraces are connected spatially and visually, while the kitchen and staff room are compartmentalised, to the rear.

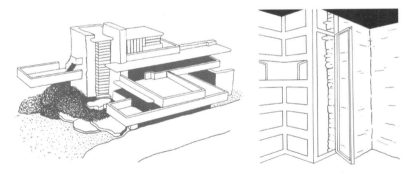

Projecting ideas

The cantilevers at Fallingwater are architectural icons in themselves, designed and stacked one above the other. Wright's design makes great use of them and their horizontal mass to create a house dominated and informed by this layering of levels.

Window on Wright

This corner window detail shows the design dexterity and craftmanship employed at Fallingwater. Notice how the tall window opens into a space cut within the desk; Wright did this when his client asked that the window be eliminated in order that the desk could be wider.

Ornamentation

Postmodern

The Vanna Venturi House (1959–64), in Chestnut Hill, Pennsylvania, was designed by Robert Venturi for his mother, Vanna. Taking reference from Modernism – note the ribbon windows – Venturi played with the design to include the dramatic broken pediment roof and slender eyebrow above the entrance, to create one of the first Postmodern homes.

Ornamentation in the form of decorative addition has been seen both as an integral part of house design in the modern era and as a petty folly. While Beaux Arts and Art Nouveau architects revelled in the chance to adorn their buildings with all manner of artistry, Modernists pushed hard for architectural forms that followed function, stripping designs of all unnecessary trim, and on the whole they won out.

Today, while mass housing schemes often hark back to Tudor, Victorian and Georgian decorative designs, the average architect has been schooled in the Modernist approach and he or she is much more inclined to look to the structural composition of a house design to beautify it. The result is a push–pull in which the homeowner is often left with the worst of both worlds.

Art Nouveau

At Hotel Tassel (1892–94), in Brussels, Belgium, the staircase of this once single home is a beautiful example of Art Nouveau design. Every aspect – from wall décor to floor tiling, balustrade and stair nosings – flows wonderfully from one perfect curve to another: art as architecture.

Future Modern

Ornamentation can take many forms and here the architect has used a grid of holes punched into the façade to enliven it from inside and out. Without this feature the end-wall might look overly imposing. However, adding the holes breaks up the massiveness of the form and also provides an interesting window style.

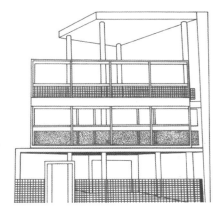

Modernist

Curutchet House (1949–53), in La Plata, Argentina, uses architectural form to intrigue, as all the best Modernist buildings do. See the doorway hovering mid-space, and the grids of brise soleil that sit in front of the windows, helping to shade the interior, while making a strong design statement, too.

Arts and Crafts

Expressing the beauty of the craftsmanship and materials being used is what Arts and Crafts design is all about, and this door and surround show just how it can be done. The woodwork is beautifully executed and the stained-glass window a masterpiece, both crafted by hand as the genre dictates.

Introduction

Home is where the art is

Casa Milà (1910) in Barcelona, Spain, is a unique and beautiful apartment building, designed by Art Nouveau architect Antoni Gaudí. The building's undulating stone façade and otherworldly wrought iron balconies are matched inside by curved walls and stair balustrades that ripple like metallic ribbons.

In the western world the Industrial Revolution was the major driver behind the construction of mass housing – homes built in close proximity to one another for large numbers of people. As factories and warehouses sprang up, business owners needed large numbers of workers living nearby in order to maintain production. They built small houses right next to the workplaces, so creating the first swathes of mass housing.

These developments set the blueprint for inner-city homes for many years to come. Today, this legacy can still be seen in the 'row' housing or back-to-back terraces that we see in many of our cities: the workers' homes of yesteryear, often becoming desirable urban dwellings of the 21st century.

However, mass housing soon moved on from these rows of small individual homes. Architects recognised the efficiencies of stacking houses on top of one another, and, twinning this ideal with new materials and techniques, such as reinforced concrete, they began to build first low-rise blocks, then mid- and finally high-rise buildings in which many people could be housed.

Initially, these buildings were styled classically, to suit the times – late 19th and early 20th centuries – but soon the Modernists took a grasp of the housing sector and their drive to build with concrete created some majestic and some monstrous mass housing schemes. The best of these buildings are still in use today, and people pay handsomely to live in them. However, poor urban planning and lack of amenities often mired the early to mid 20th-century mass housing schemes and many have since been demolished or extensively upgraded in attempts to make them livable in the 21st century.

Modernist high point
Highpoint 1 (1935), in Highgate, London, England, was designed by Russian architect Berthold Lubetkin. It contained 64 apartments within the austere white walls of a design that is still considered a fine example of International Style architecture.

Archetypes

Modernist

Karl Marx Hof (1930)
is a giant early
Modernist tenement
block, built to house
5,000 people, on the
outskirts of Vienna,
Austria. It has Art Deco
traits, but its designer
Karl Ehn was a
follower of the Garden
City Movement, an
ideal supported by
many Modernists.

Mass housing does not always mean giant blocks of apartments. Architects have designed many different types, from vast estates, or subdivisions, of almost identical individual homes, to clusters of duplex apartments and high towers.

However, the common thread running throughout these designs is density – the number of people who can be housed within a relatively small area. This is the key to mass housing and its success, or failure, in the eyes of the developer and the user. A well-designed mass housing scheme will accommodate its users comfortably and provide for their needs; a poorly designed project will soon make its users miserable.

Beaux Arts

Named due to its style, the Beaux Arts
Building, London, England (1908–11), is
a fine example of the redbrick and limestone
architecture that is still widely found in
many of the streets in English cities today.
Classical detailing around the entrances and
the large broken pediment above the arched
window make for an impressive design.

Deck access buildings

This central courtyard of a mass housing
scheme reveals the external corridors
that run the length of each storey of the
building, linking homes with stairways
and lifts on each floor. This feature is
known as deck access, and is synonymous
with many mid-rise housing schemes
around the world.

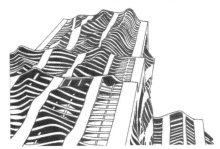

Future Modern

A skyscraper set amidst the towering office
spires of Manhattan, New York City, United
States, 8 Spruce Street (2006–10) is
architect Frank Gehry's first mass housing
project, and it is typically extravagant. The
building is home to luxury apartments,
which are wrapped in an undulating skin
of shiny stainless steel.

Mass medium-rise housing

This is a prime example of mass housing
built throughout Europe in the 1950s.
Following the Second World War, homes
were needed quickly and these large
mid-rise housing estates were built with
little concern for access to amenities or
quality of life. Today, they are often ghettos,
where only the poorest in society live.

Archetypes

Art Deco

Embassy Court (1936), in Brighton, England, is a listed apartment building overlooking the South Coast. Designed in the Art Deco style, as evident by the stepped-back upper storeys and beautifully curved windows on the front corner, it is now one of the city's most coveted places to live.

As mentioned, mass housing comes in different types. One of the most prevalent in the United States is the subdivision – sprawling developments of low-rise homes that surround the outskirts of most towns and cities. The built environment of the United States has grown in this way due to its geographical scale and the availability of land. Conversely, locations such as Singapore, Japan or Hong Kong have very few low-rise developments and their residents are housed in apartments that reach skywards.

Which of these types of home is better for the occupant is debatable. However, in each case the people concerned have been raised knowing only one thing and so expect to live in a ranch house or high-rise, respectively. The architect's job has always been to facilitate this in the best way possible.

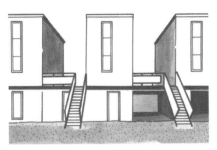

Half a house

In Chile, the concept of buying half a house and building the remainder to suit is being developed. Elemental is a project in which the service-heavy parts – kitchen, bathroom, laundry – are built by the developer and then the owner fills in the space that is left with their own bedrooms etc.

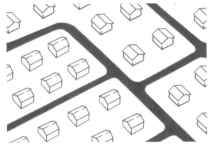

Mass low-rise housing

This aerial view of an American suburb illustrates the archetypal layout of such developments throughout the United States. The detached homes all have a driveway and are surrounded by a lawn. Adjacent houses are not exactly the same in design but throughout the development there are just a few different models.

Brutalist modern

Architects Chamberlin, Powell and Bon designed the Barbican estate in London, England, as a neighbourhood within the city, complete with shops, a school and cultural elements. Residents live in mid-rise and high-rise blocks hewn from rough concrete in a stunning example of Brutalist architecture.

Condos

The condominium is a concept developed for luxury inner-city living. Here, in Dubai, a forest of condo towers overlook the harbour, offering prime views, at high level and higher prices. Each residence within these towers is designed with every luxury in mind.

Materials and construction

Modern mastery
Designed by Moshe Safdie, for Expo 67 in Montreal, Canada, Habitat 67 (1967) is a unique housing development built from 354 identical precast concrete boxes. Arranged in groups of one to eight, these boxes make up 146 living modules, all of which include a private terrace.

Mass housing was developed by factory owners and other private-sector individuals to accommodate workers near to their place of employment. As a result it was built using the least expensive and most abundant materials. This ideal has prevailed in all but a relatively few cases – such as luxury condominiums.

With this in mind, construction materials and methods gravitated towards designs that encourage repetition and quick completion. This suited Modernist architects well and they sought to design using concrete to create often giant housing developments that would become home to many hundreds of people.

Bygone brick (right)

Tenement or terraced housing was one of the original forms of mass housing. These terraces were built back to back, with narrow laneways running between the backyards. Built towards the end of the 19th century, these homes were the precursor to the mass housing developments of today.

Making space (left)

The Baronbackarna Complex, in Orebro, Sweden, was designed by White Architects in 1951. Its success as a good mass development has been attributed to the inclusion of ample outdoor pedestrian space – gardens, pathways, cycleways and so on – which encourage inhabitants to come together as a community.

Wood is good (right)

Today, architects are looking to more sustainable resources than concrete to build housing developments, and wood is becoming more commonly used. This project in Austria is clad in wood and also structurally framed in the material, too.

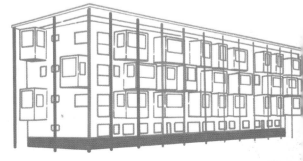

Materials and construction

Futuristic giant
Simmons Hall (1999–2002) at MIT in Cambridge, Massachusetts, United States, is student housing on a grand scale. Designed by Steven Holl, the building contains 350 residences, plus a theatre and restaurant. Each room has multiple square windows, while corridors feature organically shaped openings that bring the building façade alive.

Whether worker housing, public housing or accommodation for temporary residents such as students, mass housing has been and still is most often designed to a limited budget. That said, people nevertheless expect architects to produce something noteworthy – and so even the least expensive designs must engage their users.

Different techniques have been used to do this throughout the modern era but form and colour are by far the most commonly used. The introduction of a quirk such as a round window opening, or the addition of cladding that breaks up a giant façade into coloured bands enlivens even the most prosaic of designs at little extra cost. The benefits can be priceless, its impact lifting the design and turning a monolithic block into a place that enchants its inhabitants.

Going green

BedZed (2000-02) is the quirky name of an eco-friendly housing estate in the south of England. Designed by Bill Dunster Architects, the terraced homes feature glazed winter gardens that collect heat in the winter and large coloured ventilation cowls on the roof. The project is one of the first of its kind to be carbon neutral.

New skin, old block

Recladding an existing residential tower is one of the quickest and least expensive solutions to upgrading tired housing stock. The cladding adds extra weather protection and insulation to the exterior, while giving the building a new look, too.

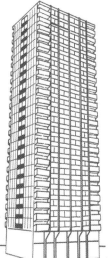

High times

Built in the early 1970s, this high-rise housing tower is a feature that most people in the United Kingdom recognise as part of their cityscapes. Built using precast concrete and infill panels, the towers were quick to erect but soon became eyesores and uncomfortable to live in as they deteriorated.

Russian roulette

This huge building is a mixed-use development built during Russia's communist era. It features homes on the upper storeys and shops and fast-food restaurants below. The design is Brutalist in form and a common sight throughout the country and much of eastern Europe.

Unité d'Habitation

With 337 apartments arranged over 12 storeys, Unité d'Habitation (1952) in Marseille, France, is not the biggest apartment block but it is one of the most influential and famous. Designed by Le Corbusier, the Modernist building, also known as *la Cité Radieuse* ('the Radiant City'), is built on the principle that it would be a self-contained city. There is a restaurant, an internal street of shops and a doctor's surgery within the building, as well as leisure facilities on the roof.

Internally, access to the apartments is via corridors on every third floor. The apartments are laid out on two levels, which stretch across the width of the building, allowing light at both ends of their home.

Coloured judgement

Unité d'Habitation's austere concrete structure and façade is broken up by coloured panels within the balconies of each apartment. Le Corbusier was assisted by artist/architect Nadir Afonso on the design and these were his influence.

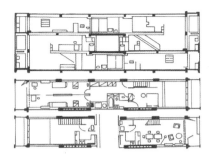

Apartment layout

Set within this diagram are two apartments, each accessed from the central core corridor. The upper apartment runs the full width of the building across the top level, plus the right-hand portion of the middle floor; the lower apartment, across the lowest storey and the left-hand midsection.

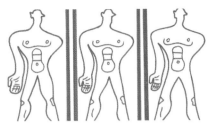

Mystery man

Set into the concrete wall of Unité is Modulor Man. This relief is more than an artwork, though, it is Le Corbusier's measuring stick for design. The architect developed 'the Modulor' as a proportional measuring tool based upon a male 1.83 m (6 ft) tall. He then used the figure as a yardstick when designing buildings and interiors.

Up on the roof

The building features a running track, children's art school and paddling pool, and a large free-standing vertical wall, which acts as stage backdrop and surface on which to project movies. Le Corbusier wanted for the inhabitants to use every inch of the building.

Middle street

The two-storey internal street includes a bookshop, grocer's and a doctor's surgery, as well as office space for small companies, including an architect. Le Corbusier meant to design a city within a city for his residents.

Doors and windows

The purely functional role of the door and window openings in our buildings is obvious: to provide for the entry and exit of the inhabitants and allow views out from and natural light into the interior spaces. In this respect, Modernist buildings do just that and often little more – their lack of whimsical ornamentation rendering the doors and windows plain and devoid of any unnecessary features.

On the other hand, the openings in the building skin are opportunities to enliven the architectural design of a building and so accentuating them in some way is the perfect way to make a façade 'pop' without adding ornament for ornament's sake. This section will illustrate some of the ways in which architects use doors and windows to their advantage on a large scale in mass housing.

Playful approach

The Waldspirale (2000), in Darmstadt, Germany is a housing complex designed by artist Friedensreich Hundertwasser. Its Avant Garde style is punctuated by more than one thousand windows, no two of which are the same. And, every door has a different style handle.

Curvaceous Deco

Florin Court (1936) stands in East London, England, the highest of the buildings surrounding Charterhouse Square. The Art Deco building has a wonderful curving façade, around which large windows curve in both concave and convex forms.

Contemporary glazing

This student housing in Denmark has no bespoke window or door elements but the architect has used them to punctuate a façade that pops back and forth. The result is an eye-catching design in which the floor-to-ceiling windows are the stars of the show.

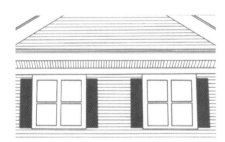

Classical aspirations

The architect of this brand-new housing development in the United States has taken inspiration for his design from classical buildings. Both the windows and doors are designed with small-pane windows – the type common in the 18th and 19th centuries.

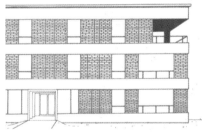

Making a Modern entrance

Far from being extrovert, this entrance to a modern apartment block is discreet, an opening tucked into a recess in the building's façade. However, the architect has cleverly picked out the doorway with the white surround, which differentiates it from the windows.

Doors and windows

The sheer number of windows required in any mass housing project is phenomenal. Architects, whether Modernists, classicists or adherents to genres in between, tend to opt for standard sizes when designing window openings, frame types and hardware.

This standardisation brings with it a uniformity that is well liked by Modernist architects. It promotes their industrialised roots and ideals, while keeping costs and construction methods to a minimum. That said, there is always the exception, like the Waldspirale (page 98) but most of the time even Postmodern housing, such as Opus in Hong Kong, tends towards standardisation of windows and doors.

Do the twist

Opus (2102), a housing development designed by Frank Gehry in Hong Kong is a twisting tower that defies architectural classification. However, while the building itself is quite unique, Gehry has opted to standardise the doors and window throughout the design, thus making the build less expensive.

Brutal beauty

Designed by Patrick Hodgson in the 1960s, London's Brunswick Centre features glazed winter gardens in all of its apartments. Like mini-greenhouses, built into each home, these unusual windowed rooms provide light-filled spaces in the Brutalist building.

Classical statement

This corner building in Spain is a wonderful example of Beaux Arts architecture that uses all of the stylistic potential that a genre built on quirkiness allows. The door and windows change style with each storey of the building, making for a statement piece of urban architecture.

Oddball architecture (left)

What can be said about the façade and windows of Le Viaduc et le Temple (1982), in Paris, France? The windows are set in a façade that is a riot of patterns and textures, and also two egg-shaped protrusions. The design is like no other, mixing classical forms with Postmodern quirks: the success of the resulting façade ... make up your own mind.

VM Houses

Spiky proposition

With modern materials and new techniques architects can achieve all sorts of wild designs and VM Houses certainly fits into that category. The apartment buildings are enlivened by triangular balconies that stick out from the building, almost defying gravity.

This extraordinary mass housing development is called VM Houses (2004–05) and it is located in Copenhagen, Denmark. The name is derived from the footprint of the two blocks – in the shape of a V and an M – and the project was designed by Danish firm JDS Architects.

In a way similar to Le Corbiusier's Unité d'Habitation, the apartments within the blocks stretch the entire width of the buildings, allowing light in at both ends. In all, there are 209 dwellings within the two blocks, including more than 80 different layouts – from small to large – to suit all requirements.

The Future Modern styling of the architecture is both fantastical and practical, directing eyelines and views towards the landscape, rather than directly at another apartment.

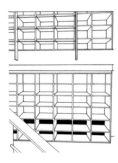

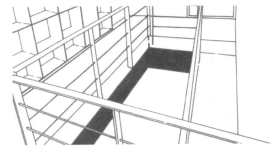

Built-in storage

Space is always an issue in compact apartment buildings but by building it into the design the architect has maximised the living area in the apartments and in doing so also created an interesting internal aesthetic.

Duplex living

Somehow a set of stairs makes a place feel a whole lot bigger. These apartments are almost all duplexes, giving a sense of height and space to what are really relatively small dwellings.

Point of Privacy (below)

The balconies not only look good but also encourage inhabitants to look out past their immediate surroundings and to the distant landscape, creating a distraction from the high-density living that is a necessity in today's urban society.

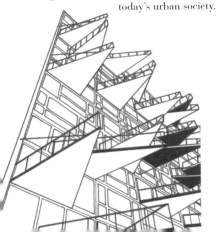

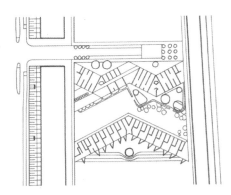

VM layout (above)

Seen in plan view, the name of the two blocks can be fully appreciated. If they were two rectilinear buildings facing each other the sense of space that the architect has engendered would be totally lost. Instead, a little forethought produces intelligent design.

Ornamentation

Making an Expression
Het Schip (1919),
in Amsterdam,
Netherlands, was
designed by Michel de
Klerk. The architect's
Expressionist style has
produced a housing
scheme, with 102
homes, that is full of
style and quirky design
surprises, such as this
beautiful spire.

How to take what is essentially a giant stack of homes and make them pretty, or cool, or simply less ugly? This is the question that designers have been asking for many years now because, as seen in many mid-20th-century housing developments, making these often huge buildings look something other than institutional is not that easy.

But architects are an ingenious bunch, and their allegiance to various genres has produced a variety of ideas when it comes to the ornamentation of mass housing schemes. Additionally, today they are very aware that those aforementioned 'institutional' 1950s developments quickly fell out of favour because they lacked flair, individuality and creativity. Newer mass housing schemes are more human in scale, and easier on the eye.

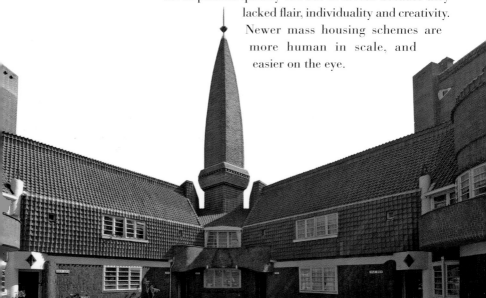

Colourful skin

This housing scheme named Arc en Ceil, in Bordeaux, France, is wrapped in a skin of coloured glass brise soleil, which works to shade the apartments from the sun and provide for a rainbow of colour on the façade.

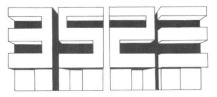

Monumental number

Taking the house number as a motif is a different approach, but it is just what happened in 2007 at Hozumidai House, Osaka, Japan which are a series of apartments designed by Mitsutomu Matsumani Architects & Associates.

Inspired by nature

Taking reference from surroundings and natural materials, Plasma Studio designed this apartment block in the Dolomite Mountains, Italy. The form is reminiscent of mountains and the cladding is predominantly locally sourced larch.

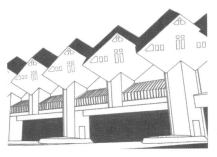

Form as decoration

Taking the building form and subverting it makes for surprising and eye-catching results, such as Cube Houses (1977), Rotterdam, Netherlands, by Piet Blom. Some 39 homes sit on hexagonal columns, their walls tilted at almost impossible angles.

Introduction

Long before houses, museums and office buildings were elevated to the iconic by exciting and statement-making architecture, the worship building was the centre of attention for master builders and architects. The church, synagogue, mosque, temple or chapel was seen as the epicentre of almost every village or town and the most important building within the community. And, due to this importance, the buildings were the most impressive to be built.

In classical architectural churches, cathedrals and temples soared, their stone walls massive, their towers, spires and domes dominating the skyline for miles around; no building was allowed to be built taller or grander than them. In the Western world architectural styles such as Roman, Gothic and Baroque produced some of the most impressive buildings ever built, many of which still stand today; while in the East a different set of religions – Buddhism, Hinduism, Islam and so on – provided contrasting inspiration and so drew disparate styles from the designers of religious buildings.

However, as the modern era dawned, and the last classically inspired churches were built, attitudes to the way that religious buildings looked began to change. Architects dared to design places of worship in a new style, moving away from tradition, from the spires and domes, cruciform footprints and processional entrances, to instil new ideals on the most ancient beliefs.

Some buildings failed, their designs too radical, too divorced from what people could connect to as their place of worship. However, skilled architects managed to design with Modernism in mind while still creating buildings that glorified the deity being worshipped; their buildings looked nothing like a traditional church but nevertheless spoke to the worshippers in a language they understood and to which they could relate.

The religious building was changed forever by Modernism – so much so that some might say that architecture had become a religion in itself.

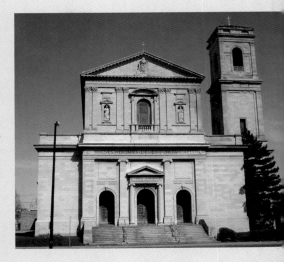

Last hurrah
St Gerard's Church (1911), in Buffalo, United States, is a fine example of classical religious architecture, and the influence that it still had at the start of the 20th century. The building is imposing yet restrained – Renaissance Revival architecture at its best.

Archetypes

Archetypal religious architecture has as much to do
with the religion involved as it does the geographic
location or the style preferred by the architect because
iconography is dependent upon its religion.

This is demonstrated when looking at almost any
religious building from the classical period and before:
Christian buildings tend towards spires and towers;
Hindu temples use domes; Muslim places of worship
have pinnacles and minarets, and so on. However, as
the modern era progressed architects took
religious design to new stylistic heights and
managed to combine faith-based symbols
with ever more radical designs.

The new church, synagogue and temple is
both a challenge and a chance to take
architectural design to its most extravagant
limits, as we'll see in this section.

Brutalist

O Studio Architects from Hong Kong designed the concrete Church of the Seed (2010), on Mount Luofu, in Huizhou, China. The Brutalist building was constructed using bamboo formwork – you can see the vertical lines on the exterior.

Contemporary Modern

The Chapel of St Albert the Great, in Edinburgh was designed by Simpson and Brown and completed in 2013. Stone walls hark back to historic neighbouring buildings but the low-slung roof and tree-like supports are very Modern in design.

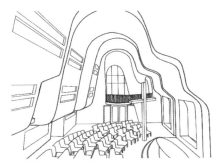

Future Modern interior

The undulating ceiling form and positioning of worshippers' chairs is like no other religious building. This is the futuristic Harajuku Church (2006), in Japan. Designed by Ciel Rouge, the ceiling form of this Protestant church is said to invoke a hand enveloping the worshippers beneath.

Modernist

Yesil Vadi Mosque (2010), in Istanbul, Turkey is unusual in many aspects but the spherical form is the most obvious of them. The white stone exterior shines brightly in the sunlight and the building's form contrasts with everything that surrounds it, making a striking addition to the cityscape.

Archetypes

Modern mosque
A fine example of
a Modernist take on
Islamic architecture,
the King Fasail Mosque
(1987), in Islamabad,
Pakistan is huge. It has
all the requisite elements
of any traditional
mosque, but the form is
unique, and has attracted
much attention.

Redesigning a building such as a church or mosque,
which has major emotional attachment for worshippers,
is not a task to be undertaken lightly. Architects walk a
fine line when designing a religious building that is
radically different from those that have come before it.
The trick is often to include within that design pattern,
form or other elements that are recognised by and
important to the user.

Additionally, when designing a religious building,
architects often reach quite literally for the sky, claiming
that their design glorifies the deity whom the users will
worship within the building. This technique has been
used throughout the ages, across the globe and all
religions. You will note that there are not many worship
buildings that are diminutive in scale or grandeur.

Arts and Crafts

Looking more like a fancy house than a church, this Arts and Crafts-style building is the First Church of Christ Scientist (1910), Berkeley, United States. Designed by Bernard Ralph Maybeck, it was listed as a US National Historic Monument in 1977.

Fusion

St Mary's Church (1937) in Causeway Bay, Hong Kong, is an example of the fusion between western construction techniques and eastern design aesthetics. The monumental red-brick walls are something not often seen in Hong Kong but their imposing nature is tempered by the Chinese-influenced tiered roofs.

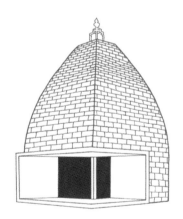

Classic form, modern ideals

This beautifully simple Shiv Temple (2010), in Maharashtra, India, designed by Sameep Padora Associates, was built by villagers using local stone and timber. The architect stripped all decoration to reduce the design to its pure, classical form.

Expressionist

The Church of Hallgrimur in Iceland is the tallest in the country. Designed by Godjon Samuelsson, it took 38 years to build, finally being completed in 1986. The unique tower is said to have been inspired by Iceland's basalt lava flows.

Materials and construction

Concrete cells
Le Corbusier designed the Monastery of St Marie de la Tourette (1956), in Eveux, France. It is similar in style to his housing projects, in that it is almost Brutal in aesthetic. Tiny bare cells for sleeping are contrasted with large open spaces for dining, all set within a concrete shell.

Religious buildings are almost always built to last; historically, they are constructed with a permanence that no other genre can match. Compare wattle and daub houses and stone churches of Tudor times – one made of wood, clay and straw, the other hewn from rocks. The latter is always going to last longer.

And, for the most part, the same has been true of churches, mosques, temples and synagogues in modern times. As new materials and techniques were developed, architects looked to them instead of the traditional. Hence, concrete became a favourite of the radical Modernist, while stone was cut differently to give new finishes and forms.

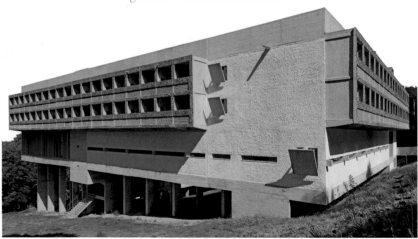

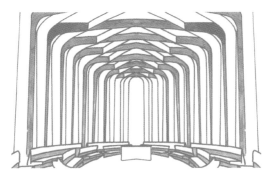

Modern arches (left)
The slender beauty of the internal framework of Bishop Edward King Chapel (2013), at Ripon College, England, makes for a wonderful sight – whether the visitor is religious or not. The arches, a traditional aspect of church architecture, are updated in the Modern design.

Steel spires (right)
The spire, another archetypal element of religious architecture, is translated here into a row of 17 tubular steel-framed elements clad in aluminium, which jut into the sky. The Air Force Academy Cadet Chapel (1962), in El Paso, Colorado, United States, was designed by Skidmore, Owings & Merrill.

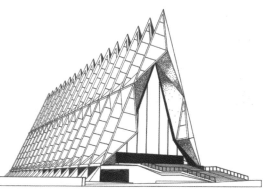

Curved concrete (left)
Three partial spheres stand together at the Jubilee Church (2003), in Rome, Italy. The precast concrete shapes were designed by Richard Meier, who says that they form part of a thermal stability strategy to keep the temperature inside the building constant and cool.

Materials and construction

Elegant glass

Wayfarers Chapel (1949–51), Rancho Palos Verdes, California, was designed by Lloyd Wright (Frank Lloyd Wright's son), and features beautiful carpentry and large transparent glass windows, which are unusual in religious buildings.

Whatever the material, the religious building has to look and feel special, even monumental. With this in mind, architects have any number of tricks and techniques to take even the most mundane of materials and create something wonderful. Concrete can be formed into almost any shape imaginable. Glass does not have to be transparent or colourless; wood can be carved into the most intricate of sculptural detail.

The construction techniques used to create some of these ideals are a combination of ancient and modern. Computer-aided design is prevalent but the 'enlightened' designer will also look to the past, when craftsmanship was at its peak, to rediscover old styles of working and bring them to new architectural design. This approach was evident in Arts and Crafts designs but it is still relevant in the newest of 21st-century buildings, too.

Material mix

The Beth Shalom Synagogue (2008), in San Francisco, United States, is a brand-new place of worship, and the architecture is radically different to prove it. Both its form and use of striking contemporary materials – metals and plastics – mark it out as 21st-century Modern.

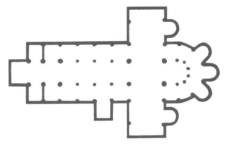

Traditional cathedral plan

Once upon a time (before the Modernist revolution) almost all churches were built to this cruciform plan. However, today churchgoers and designers have relaxed in their attitudes towards form, and churches come in many different shapes and sizes.

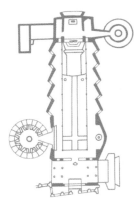

Modern cathedral plan

The footprint for Coventry Cathedral (1956–62), England, shows how Modernists subverted the cruciform plan ideal. Still rectilinear but with asymmetric elements to its exterior, the cathedral brings the cross shape inside, enabling a different approach to the building's external façade/form.

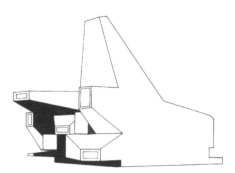

Metal religion

Designed by Vicens & Ramos Arquitectos, the Santa Monica Parish Church (2009), in Rivas Vaciamadrid, Spain, is one of the most unusual religious buildings you'll ever see. Its jutting external façade is built using panels of Corten steel, which is oxidised to give a rust-effect finish.

Unity Temple

Concrete worship

The plain grey external façade of the building may seem dowdy but it is Frank Lloyd Wright's homage to concrete, a new material that would totally change the way in which buildings were constructed.

Built between 1905 and 1908, Unity Temple, in Oak Park, United States, was one of a number of religious buildings designed by architectural superstar Frank Lloyd Wright. The building is built entirely of reinforced concrete, which at that time was a thoroughly new material, and as such, it is today lauded as a tour de force of new ideals.

Lloyd Wright designed the building with no eye-level windows to cut down on street noise. Instead, light enters via roof lights and clerestories high up in the walls. The green/brown colour scheme of the interior is said to evoke nature but the geometric designs are Lloyd Wright's trademark, and, some might say, quite Art Deco in style.

Modern columns (left)

The external decoration of the temple is almost entirely focused on the columns that run along the front façade. Geometric designs on their square sides hark back to Egyptian or Mayan patterning – the architect used such designs on many of his buildings.

Internal detailing (right)

Unity Temple is all about squares. The building is perfectly square in plan and Lloyd Wright took this motif and applied it to everything, including the interior décor. Here, square skylights in the ceiling float above wooden patterning, and bespoke light fittings with two square (and a single round) diffusers.

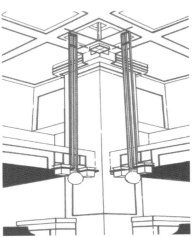

Cross-section 'thru concrete' (left)

Frank Lloyd Wright's original drawings of the temple are amazingly detailed. This one shows a section through the building. Note the dark structural elements, which are all reinforced concrete. These include the balconies and roof structure.

Doors and windows

Glorious glass

Completed in 2008, the Cathedral of Christ the Light, in Oakland, California, is a Modernist Roman Catholic church designed by Skidmore, Owings & Merrill. Almost all of the building's external façade is glass; it is one giant window.

From ancient to classical times and into the modern era, the entrance into a space believed by worshippers to be filled with the presence of a god has always been a special doorway. The windows, said by some to allow divine light to pour into the interior, have also been marked out for special treatment in architectural terms.

Architects in the 20th century did not feel compelled to copy older styles when designing doors and windows in religious buildings; ensuring that their genre of choice left its mark, especially at these critical elements in the buildings. In fact, the apertures within these places of worship were the perfect place to make a statement.

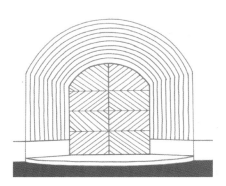

Classic Nouveau

Grundtvigs Church, in Copenhagen, Denmark, was completed in 1940. It is a Lutheran church and a great example of Expressionist architecture. The doorway is shaped like a classical Roman arch but the brickwork detailing, door construction and handle are all Modern-influenced.

Organic inspiration

A new take on the pictorial leaded glass windows (often with stained glass in them), the Lilja Chapel of Silence, built as a temporary structure in 2012 in Finland, features a glazed end wall that is inspired by the form of a tree. The design focuses on the beauty of nature.

Modern processional entrance

The entrance to Liverpool Metropolitan Cathedral (1962–67) is a modern take on the classical stairway that leads to many large cathedrals of all styles all over the world. The architect makes use of an age-old element in this radical Postmodern design.

Transparent ribbon

Light floods into the worship space of the Chapel del Retiro (2009), in Chile, via a transparent wall of glass, over which the upper portion of the building floats. The design by Undurraga Deves Arquitectos seems to defy gravity.

Doors and windows

WORSHIP

Making a point

The diminutive Bruder Klaus Field Chapel (2007), designed by Peter Zumthor, is a Minimalist design whose only outward adornment is this unusual triangular door. The door itself is not very large but its impact upon the design is massive, thanks to the architect's paired-down design.

Both doors and windows can be about so much more, especially in worship buildings. Unless the building design is really unusual the actual entrance is most often designed on a size that we relate to rather than being massive. However, what architects did in classical times and continued to do into the Modern era was accentuate the size of the entrance with a dramatic surround. Arched surrounds were a traditional favourite, building out and up from the doorway itself. Similarly, window surrounds increase the perceived size of the window making them seem much more dramatic: the result, supersized doorways and windows for the religious buildings that are so important to so many people.

Postmodern stained glass

Here the traditional stained-glass window is updated in a Postmodern style at Old St Patrick's (1856), in Chicago, United States. Classical themes are retold with a twist in this gloriously quirky stained-glass design.

Renaissance Revival doorways

Completed in 1913, St Gerard's, Buffalo, United States is a Renaissance Revival church that is sticking with the classical tradition we have come to associate with much religious architecture. The arches, pilasters and pediments could very well be adorning an 18th-century building.

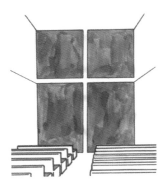

Religious iconography

Here, the very symbolism that the Christian faith is built around is used as a window into the building. At the Church of the Light (1989) in Ibaraki, Japan, the cross form is the only aperture in the end wall of the building, with dramatic consequences.

Modern interpretation

Subverting the norm, the Wat Anada Metyarama Buddhist temple (2014) in Thailand the windows are a plethora of triangular apertures punched out of the walls. The temple was designed by Singapore practice Czarl Architects.

Chapel of Notre Dame du Haute

Religious designs

Built high on a hillside, the Chapel of Notre Dame du Haut is a piece of architectural sculpture. No two walls are the same and windows seem to be randomly scattered across the façade. The concrete roof billows, like a sail in the wind, its edge seeming to lift off from the white walls.

The Chapel of Notre Dame du Haut, in Ronchamp, France, was completed in 1954. Designed by Franco-Swiss architect Le Corbusier, it replaces an original chapel that was destroyed during the Second World War.

The structure of the building is mainly concrete, with the walls as much as 3 m (10 ft) thick in places. These super-thick walls are constructed of two 'skins', between which is rubble from the debris of the original chapel.

The building's form is unique, not referencing any other building or genre. Critics describe the chapel as the first Postmodern building, but Le Corbusier was not attempting to subvert his Modernist ideals; he was simply experimenting with light and form.

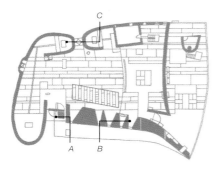

Plan layout

To the bottom of the image is the super-thick south wall (A), and to its left side the main entrance (B). At the top are the curved forms that appear as towers (C), and which enclose small chapels within the main building.

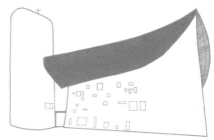

Oversailing roof

The roof is concrete like the rest of the building but it is left bare, rather than being sprayed with mortar and painted white. Le Corbusier modelled it on the shell of a crab and its oversailing elements shelter a small outdoor chapel.

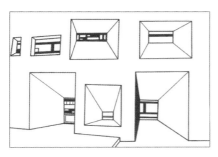

Super-thick wall

Within the wall are punched window openings. Within these openings are windows containing coloured glass in the architect's trademark red, yellow and green. Light shining through them bounces colours off the interior walls.

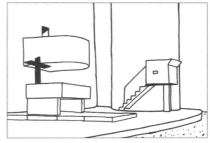

Outdoor chapel

The eastern façade of the building is the backdrop to a small outdoor chapel. Le Corbusier designed a pulpit, table and simple metal cross, which form this external worship space tucked discreetly beneath the eaves of the dramatic concrete roof.

Ornamentation

Renaissance glamour
Arches, columns, a fresco, a coffered ceiling and even a giant alcove in which the altar resides, all go to create a religious statement at St Adalbert Church (1912), in Chicago, United States. The Roman Catholic church stands in an historic Polish neighbourhood, and features both religious and Polish ornamentation.

There is perhaps no other building type better suited to the integration of ornamentation than the religious building. Every religion has one or more symbols, patterns or iconic figures that architects have been working into the building design for aeons.

The difference between ancient, classical and modern architecture is that more recent styles tended towards the minimalisation of ornament; how did architects reinvent the glorification of buildings that visitors expected to be shrines to a variety of gods?

The answers are many and varied, beginning in the late 19th and early 20th centuries with architects clinging to classical motifs. As time went on, new but still evocative designs came to be loved by the public.

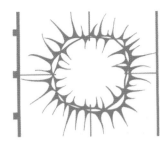

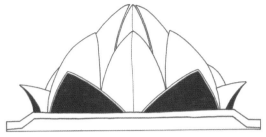

Modernist art

An iron crown of thorns frames the image of an angel in the Gethsemane Chapel, at Coventry Cathedral (1956–62). The cathedral, partially destroyed during the Second World War, was rebuilt in a Modernist style and the artworks reflect the genre, too.

Organic form

The Lotus Temple (1986), in New Delhi, India, is perhaps one of the best examples of organic architecture ever built. Its form, modelled from the petals of a lotus flower, is a giant facsimile of the plant itself.

Fantastic façade

The dramatic façade of the Neue Synagogue (2010), in Mainz, Germany, is a statement in itself. The building behind is less exciting but the façade, built out of glazed ceramic tiles, brings attention back to the Jewish community in the area, which was once one of the most important in Germany.

No ornamentation

Making a statement by stripping its interior of anything that might be called ornamentation, Setre Chapel (2005) in Kobe, Japan, was designed by Ryuichi Ashizawa Architects & Associates. Its Minimalist design is meant to invoke meditation on the spiritual.

Introduction

With almost every building type, architects had the luxury of taking experience and reference from those who had designed and built before them. However, tall buildings – and by tall we mean higher than your average church spire and including multiple storeys –

did not really exist before the invention of structural steel. Before then, stone was the structural material of choice and the only way of building high was by making a massive foundation and extremely thick walls on the lower storeys. This type of construction created towers of a 'wedding cake' style – their lower tiers being big and wide, the upper ones getting progressively smaller as they rose.

However, just before the turn of the 20th century architects began to build with steel. They found that they could

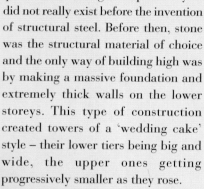

Modern classic
PPG Place in Pittsburgh was completed in 1984. Designed by Philip Johnson and John Burgee, the collection of six glass-clad buildings, including the 40-storey tower, are an extravagant Postmodern play on the Neo-Gothic architecture of the past.

design super-strong structures that were the same size at the top as they were at street level. This meant that buildings within crowded cities could rise up further without taking up any more space at ground level.

These new tall buildings were not very high by today's standards but they towered above the cityscape of the 1890s and 1900s. Style-wise, architects were still predominantly influenced by classical architecture and the new towers were adorned with Renaissance Revival or Beaux Arts ornamentation. However, beneath their classical skin there lay the bones of a brave new age of architecture, an advance from which we have never looked back and which now has architects vying to build the first ever mile-high tower.

Fantastic futuristic

At 321 m (1,053 ft) tall, the Burj al Arab, in Dubai, is three times as tall as the Sun Tower (Page 18). Completed in 1999, the sail-shaped hotel tower is built on an artificial island just off the coast of Dubai. It has more than 200 rooms and a helipad on the roof

TALL

Archetypes

Tall buildings are a relatively new invention in terms of architectural history, but a surprising proportion of them are designed with a classical twist. Both Renaissance Revival and Beaux Arts designs are common, as are Gothic-inspired creations. However, as the 20th century gained momentum, and the ravages of the First World War receded into the past, a new era of Art Deco skyscrapers began. These were the first truly tall buildings and they include such iconic buildings as the Empire State Building and Chrysler Building, both in New York City.

Since then, other countries have taken over the contest of vying for tallest in the world – and other styles have become prominent. The sheer glass of Internationalism was dominant for a long time, but today architects are opting to wow us once again with ever more elaborate forms and façade treatments.

Art Deco

The Chrysler Building (1928–30), in Manhattan, New York City, is perhaps one of the most famous skyscrapers in history. Designed by William Van Alen, the Art Deco behemoth is steel-framed but clad in brick – apart from its metal spire, which was hoisted up in sections through the inside of the building.

International

The Richard J. Daley Center, in Chicago, United States, was designed by C. F. Murphy Associates and completed in 1965. Its façade of Corten steel and dark-tinted glass give it a monochromatic look that suited the Modernist/Internationalist ideals of the time.

Postmodern

Less a skyscraper, more a giant office building, Number One Poultry, in London, England, is a wedge-shaped delight of Postmodern architecture. Clad in pink and yellow limestone, the building was designed by James Stirling and completed in 1997, five years after his death.

Deconstructivist

Architect Paul Rudolph designed the Lippo Center (1988), in Hong Kong, in response to the swathes of austere, sheer-walled towers in the city. His deconstructed façade sees pods of windows protruding, to break up the volume of the building.

Expressing religion

This Catholic church tower in Gelsenkirchen, Germany was designed by Josef Frank in 1927. It has a degree of classical form but its massive stone bulk and contrasting delicate stone decoration are evidence of an architect moving into a new and 'expressive' design period.

Archetypes

Traditionally, there were two predominant types of tall building, the office tower and the high-rise hotel. Both require mass duplication of the same type of room or space, making them easy to design and 'stack' vertically. However, in recent years architects have been charged with contributing to the intensification of 24-hour use of our cities, and mixed-use tall buildings have become the norm. These will often feature retail space on the lowest floors, office space above and then leisure, hotel and even private accommodation above that. Finally, the towers often include a public viewing deck at or near the top of the building to attract tourists. Skyscrapers have become microcosms of the city in which they reside.

Modern

Designed by I. M. Pei, the Bank of China Tower (1985–89), in Hong Kong, is 367.4 m (1,205.4 ft) tall at its highest point and was inspired by growing bamboo shoots. The building is partially supported by the space frame that can be seen on the outside.

Future Modern

Designed by Renzo Piano, The Shard (2013), in London, England, is Europe's tallest building, standing 306 m (1,004 ft) tall. Clad totally in glass, the building is designed to blend into the skyline rather than make a mark upon it, due to its position within the historical centre of the city.

Folly

London's ArcelorMittal Orbit was designed especially for the 2012 Olympic Games, by artist Anish Kapoor and architect/engineer Cecil Balmond. It stands 114 m (374 ft) high and has two viewing decks to give visitors a bird's eye view over the Olympic Park.

Art Nouveau

The Wedding Tower was designed by Joseph Maria Olbrich in 1905 to commemorate the marriage of Ernst-Ludwig, Grand Duke of Hesse, to Princess Eleonore of Solms-Hohensolms-Lich. The red-brick tower has five tile-covered spires at its peak to signify it as the crowning glory of Darmstadt, Germany.

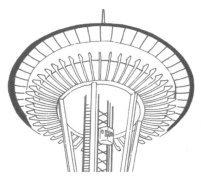

Viewing platform

The Space Needle (1961), in Seattle, United States, and CN Tower (1973–76), in Toronto, Canada, are remarkably similar in design. Both were built as viewing platforms over their respective cities and each features express elevators running up a reinforced concrete column to a revolving restaurant on the top levels.

Materials and construction

Three things governed the development of truly tall buildings – those taller than about ten storeys – and they were: structural material; means of access to the upper floors; and the ability to supply water to those

topmost floors. The last of these three was overcome some time before the other two but it was not until the latter part of the 19th century that properly functional lifts (elevators) were invented. Couple this overcoming of access problems with the fact that structural steel came on the scene at around the same time and the first skyscrapers were born.

The ten-storey Home Insurance Building, in Chicago, was the world's first to feature a structural steel frame that supported the entire weight of the building. Designed by William Le Baron Jenney, it was completed in 1885.

Steel and stone

From the Home Insurance Building things just got taller. The Empire State Building, in New York City, United States, was the tallest building in the world on completion in 1931. Its steel-frame skeleton is clad in brick and stone.

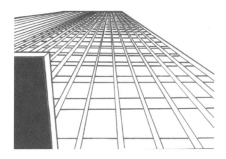

Refining steel and glass

Ludwig Mies van der Rohe designed the Seagram Building (1958), in New York City, United States. Its monolithic appearance is due to the architect's stripped-down design of steel and glass, making it a true Modernist, even Minimalist, landmark.

New structural ideas

Architects always push boundaries. The Cayan Tower (2006–13), in Dubai, is a twisted version of the conventional apartment tower. Designed by Skidmore, Owings & Merrill, the tower twists through 90 degrees as it ascends its 73 floors and 306 m (1,004 ft) in height.

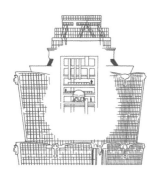

Wind factors

The giant ball in the centre of this image is the tuned mass damper used to counteract wind loading on Taipei 101 (1999–2003), in Taiwan. As the wind pushes the tower in one direction the massively heavy ball acts like a pendulum, swinging the opposite way, to minimise movement on the tower.

Tall wood

Steel is not the only structural material available to today's architects. Here, two designs for structural wood cores to tall buildings are shown. The taller one has structural partition walls and glulam beams in addition to a structural core, adding strength.

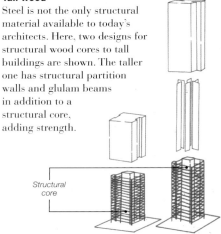

Structural core

Materials and construction

Number 30 St Mary Axe (2001–04) in London, England, is nicknamed 'the Gherkin' due to its shape. The tower, designed by Foster + Partners, features a raft of environmental ideas, including gaps in each floor that create shafts to aid natural venting and allow warm, stale air to rise and escape.

The curtain wall is one of the most significant advances in recent architectural history and it has been used to maximum effect on tall buildings. Essentially, it is a non-structural façade that is hung from the external edges of the building. Typically, curtain walls are made out of extruded aluminium frames and glass panels, but they can include composite, insulated panels or even concrete infill panels, which tend to sit in between the structural floor slabs of the building.

International Style architecture was the first genre really to integrate the curtain wall into its 'pattern book', though there were offices in the United States and the United Kingdom that used a version of the technique as early as the start of the 20th century.

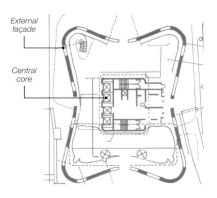

External skeleton

The plan view of this building shows that there are no internal columns and that it is supported entirely by the central core and the external façade or skeleton. This makes for large uninterrupted spaces in the building, and flexible layouts.

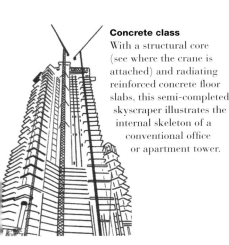

Concrete class

With a structural core (see where the crane is attached) and radiating reinforced concrete floor slabs, this semi-completed skyscraper illustrates the internal skeleton of a conventional office or apartment tower.

Sunny side up

Torre Mayor (2003–10) is Mexico's tallest building and it is also one of its most energy efficient. One of the most prominent energy-reduction techniques found in the building is its semi-solid façade on the north (sun-facing) side. This reduces solar gain within the building, keeping it cooler.

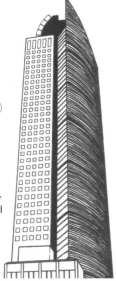

High-rise living

One of the most densely populated cities on earth, Hong Kong, has a multitude of high-rise towers, used as workplaces, hotels and, here, housing. While architects and governments call for more urban densification, this takes the idea beyond its limits and the consequences are yet to be really felt.

Bankers Trust Building

This unusual office building was built by American architect Trowbridge & Livingston between 1910 and 1912. Its style is neoclassical in style – an offshoot of the Renaissance Revival movement – with Italian influences, including the pyramidal structure, or ziggurat, on the top, which is similar to that on St Mark's Campanile in Venice.

The classical style of the building can be seen in its façade, which takes the form of an ancient column, with three elements – the base (the lower storeys), midsection or shaft, and capital. However, the fact that this building is Modern can easily be proven by its height and sheer façade. No ancient or classical-period tower could achieve this.

Classical ideals

The Bankers Trust Building was one of the last of an era. Its classically inspired façade is a joy to behold, since there are so many references to ancient and Roman architecture. The building even features two colonnades, one at the base and one near the top.

Pyramidal crown

Crowning a tall building with a pyramid, or ziggurat, is unusual in today's architectural styles but in the early 20th century such adornments were common. This one is said to have been inspired by the Mausoleum of Halicarnassus, a Greek tomb from 350BCE.

Cornice detail

The cornice splits the building façade at about the sixth-floor level, giving the design a detailing that is meant to connect with the street on a more human scale. Trowbridge & Livingston recognised that this tall building needed grounding and the cornice accentuates the base, setting up the aesthetic to soar to the pointed tip.

Columns and colonnades

Near road-level the building's façade looks to be supported by a row of four columns on each of its sides. The large scrolled capitals at the column heads denote them as of the Ionic order, a classical design favoured by the Greeks.

Building a monument

This image of the construction of the building illustrates excellently the steel frame that supports the entire structure. Hidden within the walls, it is the true hero of this and the majority of other tall buildings that surround the Bankers Trust Building.

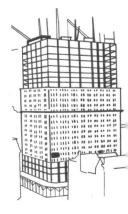

Doors and windows

On one hand, doors and windows may seem like a mere detail when considering the monumental design and construction achievements in the tall buildings sector, both today and in the past. But the window in particular is an element that helped transform skyscrapers from large stone monoliths into the light-filled towers that we know today.

With the invention of curtain walls, architects could hang glazed panels off the steel superstructure and create complete walls of glass, so offering users of tall buildings views of a kind never seen before. This also created sheer-sided towers that transformed city architecture and in so doing rocketed Modernist and Internationalist designs to the forefront of public awareness.

Full circle

Guanghzou Circle (2013), in China, is one of the most unusual tall buildings in the world. Its doughnut-like shape is matched by an unusual structural design, which is almost completely infilled with glazed panels. Designer Joseph di Pasquale has reinvented the way that we think about skyscrapers.

Patterned façade

Façade design is becoming an art in its own right and the Dear Ginza Building (2013), in Japan, is an example of how today's architects use functional elements such as façade shading to create unusual building envelopes. Designed by Amano Design Office, the glass façade is shrouded in a punched aluminium skin that looks like folded paper.

Art Deco panel

From the early 20th century onwards, Art Deco architects used artworks to glorify the entrances of tall buildings. Here, at the Dallas Power & Light Building (1930), in Dallas, Texas, United States, architect Lang & Witchell installed a glazed panel above the main entrance to great effect.

Rainscreen cladding

Renzo Piano designed the colourful façades on Central Saint Giles (2010) in central London, England, as rainscreen cladding, an outer skin that protects against the weather while allowing air to percolate up inside the façade.

Making an entrance

At QV1 (1988–91), in Perth, Australia the architect has chosen to maximise the impact felt upon entrance to the building by designing an undulating glass canopy. This technique of accentuating the building entrance is one used often by Modern architects as they seek to add interest to giant, glass-skinned towers.

Doors and windows

As the 20th century progressed, architectural styles changed and so did the entranceways into buildings – from the pillared and porticoed glamour of outgoing classical movements, to the stylised chic of Art Deco and Art Nouveau and then into the Modernist era and subgenres such as Minimalism. Architects' ideas and elaborations moved from an insistence on ornamentation around the doorway to cutting out superfluous decorative elements and even stripping almost every vestige of elaboration save for the door itself. However, this did not last, and Classical Revivalists, Expressionists and Postmodern architects turned their attention back to the entrance of a building, once again giving emphasis to the door and its surrounds, with quirks, tricks and design ideas.

Standout statement

The proliferation of arches and pediments that adorn the façade of the Continental Building, in Los Angeles, United States, is quite stunning. This Beaux Arts beauty was designed by John Parkinson and George Edwin Bergstrom in 1903 and its upper two storeys are extravagantly decorated with classically inspired forms.

Romanticised International (left)
International Style architecture can be beautiful, as proven here by the detailing to the lower floors and entrance of One M&T Bank Center (1964–66), in Buffalo, New York. The tall, graceful arches give emphasis on a human scale to the building designed by Minoru Yamasaki.

Ground-level treatment (right)
The designer of this office building in Singapore has taken a different approach to the lower two storeys than to those above, in order to make them stand out and attract passers-by. By simply glazing the façade, the architect has made the building seem open and inviting.

Postmodern giant (left)
Taking inspiration from the classical era and designing a grand, arched entrance, Philip Johnson created architectural drama at the Sony Center, in Manhattan, New York City. The building's arch towers above rectilinear glazed screens, giving emphasis and style to the entrance.

Petronas Towers

In the 20th century there was no building taller than the Petronas Towers (1993–98) in Kuala Lumpur, Malaysia. Designed by American architect Cesar Pelli, the extravagantly styled twin towers are 452 m (1,483 ft) in height and feature 32,000 windows. Their Postmodern design is influenced by Islamic architecture, with Pelli taking reference from tropical fruits and Islamic art to come up with one of the most recognisable tall buildings in the world today.

The two towers were built simultaneously and they are linked at the 41st and 42nd floors by the skybridge – the highest two-storey bridge in the world. The Petronas Towers lost their claim to tallest building in the world in 2004, when Taipei 101 was completed in Taiwan.

Slender giants

The Petronas Towers are the culmination of architect Cesar Pelli's career. He has designed many tall buildings, including towers in New York City and London, but none are taller or more extravagant. The design reflects Malaysian culture while remaining true to Pelli's Postmodernist ideals.

Islamic-inspired plan

Look at the footprint of each of the Petronas Towers and you'll see a many-pointed star. This symbol is derived from the Rub el Hizb, an Islamic form that includes two squares rotated around the same axis, with a circle inscribed in the centre.

High skybridge

The skybridge is in fact a two-storey walkway and fire-escape route connecting the 41st and 42nd floors. This is the highest point that visitors can get to in the building, which is the headquarters of a major corporation.

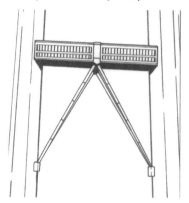

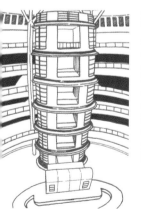

Inside the towers

The unusual shape of the towers makes for interesting architecture inside, too. The lower levels are a multi-storey shopping mall and restaurant court, which have become major tourist attractions in the Malaysian city of Kuala Lumpur.

Tall spires

Each tower is crowned with a spire, an addition that was not conceived in the original design. However, when the client realised that the building could be the tallest in the world he instructed Pelli to raise its height. The architect added a dome and an antenna.

Ornamentation

Is ornamentation important on buildings that are sometimes so tall that their tops cannot easily be seen from ground level? This is a question that architects have largely ignored for many years. Ever since skyscrapers were first built, their designers have been lavishing ornamental detail all over them, no matter the height or location.

These ornamentations differ depending upon the style to which the architect adheres, but apart from some strict Internationalist designs, nearly every truly tall building features some form of decoration. After all, these architectural giants are designed and built as totems to business and commerce, their form, height and ornamentation all part of the bragging rights of some rich corporation that is stating its claim to greatness on the world stage.

Colourful addition
Torre Agbar (2005), in Barcelona, Spain, is a phallically shaped tower designed by Jean Nouvel. By day the façade is a pixelated mix of blue and red patterning, but at night the tower's 4,500 LED arrays enable its operators to create colourful lightshows all over the building's exterior.

Terrific terracotta

The detailing at the cornices and eaves of the Guaranty Building, in Buffalo, United States, is so intricate that it can hardly be seen from the street but that evidently doesn't matter; the entire building, designed by Louis Sullivan and built in 1896, is covered in beautiful designs in terracotta.

Inspiring spire

Decking out the top of this 'wedding cake' of a building with a spire was the only way to go. The Hotel Ukraina (1957), Moscow, in Russia, is a Stalinist version of Beaux Arts architecture that rises to 206 m (676 ft) in height, including its spire.

Fusion of cultures

The unusual form of the Bank of China Tower (1985–89), in Hong Kong, is not simply a design created for Modernist times. I. M. Pei's inspiration behind the design is that of a bunch of bamboo shoots, pushing ever upwards to symbolise growth and prosperity.

Art Deco decoration

This detail of an adornment to the external façade of the RKO Building (1930–39), in New York City, is indicative of ornamentation designed for Art Deco buildings of the time. The building was home to broadcasting firm RKO and the fist holding lightning or electricity evokes the power of broadcasting.

Introduction

Art Deco power

Battersea Power Station (1933), sitting on the banks of the River Thames in London, England, is a prime example of a landmark created out of an industrial building. Designed by J. Theo Halliday and built in two phases in the 1930s and 1950s, the building is an Art Deco design in what has been dubbed Brick Cathedral style.

Our chapter on 'work' could include many and varied building types, including skyscrapers, religious buildings, theatres and educational establishments; after all, people work almost everywhere nowadays. However, we will concentrate on buildings built specifically to facilitate labour of one form or another – the powerhouses of industry and commerce.

Factories were often built with little or no architectural imagination. They were traditionally no more than large boxes in which to house a manufacturing or research process. However, when forward-thinking company owners employed architects to create something a little more interesting the results were often outstanding.

Modern era architects jumped at the chance not only to design often massive structures but also to give them personality – to make them into landmarks. Additionally, Modernists excelled at 'engineering' a building to suit the processes to be engaged in – they took their 'form follows function' mantra and ran with it to create buildings as machines.

These design considerations continue to be influential in the present day, although architects are less rigid in their Modernist philosophies and they tend to design in additional levels of comfort and relaxation space now. Work buildings still offer the designer a chance to embrace massive scale and to design something monumental. In the 1980s and 1990s architects such as Norman Foster, Nicholas Grimshaw and Renzo Piano took their High Tech style to its logical conclusion, with factories and headquarters buildings bristling with steel and wire, while newer and more advanced industry types have clamoured for architects who utilise state-of-the-art materials and techniques to create buildings that accentuate the groundbreaking work being carried out inside.

The work building could be seen as the poor relation of such grandiose structures as cathedrals and skyscrapers but in reality it is an equally exciting chance for Modern architects to stretch their design wings and create another icon.

American marvel
Frank Lloyd Wright designed the Johnson Wax Building in the late 1930s in Racine, Wisconsin, United States. Its style is typical of the architect; inside, the 'Great Work Room' is supported on slender columns that bloom into 'lily pads' at the ceiling.

Archetypes

The work building has an obvious primary function but it can also be used as a landmark or totem of recognition for the company to whom it belongs. Through the modern era and before, architects have been tasked with designing work buildings that are iconic as well as functional.

These monuments to manufacturing, power generation, public governance, finance and commerce have become architectural beacons around which many of our towns and cities evolved; they are instantly recognisable to people near and far.

But what of their style? Well, work buildings of pretty much every style have been built in cities around the world and architects have adapted even the most elaborate and whimsical designs to suit the factories, office buildings and power stations that populate our neighbourhoods.

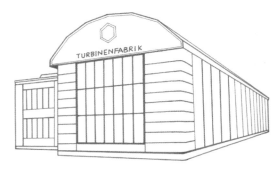

Beaux Arts

This Beaux Arts office building in Manchester, England, is now divided into multiple apartments. However, originally it was the headquarters of Lloyds Packing Warehouses Ltd. The limestone and red-brick design (1905) by Harry S. Fairhurst features a variety of window forms, different broken pediments and assorted cornice mouldings.

Early Modern

Designed by Peter Behrens, the AEG Turbine Factory in Berlin was an early example of Modernist industrial architecture in Germany. The giant building features 15-m (50-ft) high glass and steel walls, a new and exciting innovation in 1909, when the factory was built.

Art Deco

Built in Glasgow, Scotland, in 1938, the Luma Lightbulb factory became an instant landmark due to its flamboyant Art Deco design. The glass tower, evoking a light bulb, has curved walls and the thin-metal window frames associated with late Art Deco and early Modernism.

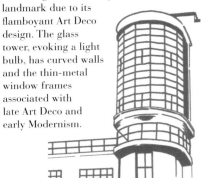

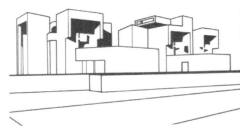

Modernist

Located in Boulder, Colorado, the Mesa Laboratory of the National Center for Atmospheric Research (1964–67) was designed by architect I. M. Pei. Its unfinished concrete walls and 'stacked-block' form are attempts to complement and contrast with the rugged surrounding landscape.

Archetypes

Modern

The Lingotto Factory (1916–23), in Turin, Italy, was designed by Matté Trucco for car manufacturer Fiat. The five-storey building has a continuous ramp connecting every floor. Car parts go in at the base of the building and finished cars come out onto a test track at the top – an architectural production line, no less.

Modernism transformed the way in which architects approached the interior layout and overall design of buildings in the work sector. Seeing that their buildings could be made more efficient, corporations employed forward-thinking designers not only to create landmarks but also to transform the working practices within.

Innovators such as Frank Lloyd Wright in the United States and Walter Gropius in Europe re-examined every aspect of industrial processes in order to design buildings that would enable employees to function at maximum efficiency. This in turn influenced the form of the structures and created a new architectural ideal within the industrial and commercial world.

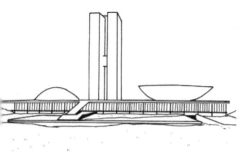

International

One of Oscar Niemeyer's iconic structures within the city of Brasilia, the National Congress Building (1957–64) is an architectural statement of intent for Brazil. Its forms – low-slung, high-tower and double domes – are both functional and architecturally stunning.

High Tech

The Willis Building (1970–75), in Ipswich, England, was one of the first buildings designed by Norman Foster's firm, Foster + Partners. Built in the High Tech style, its interior is dominated by the delicate latticework of steel beams, held up on concrete columns at the building's perimeter.

Postmodern

Designed by Michael Graves, the postmodern Portland Building (1982), in Portland, United States, is a reaction against the lack of design flamboyance of many Modernist buildings. This large office building features coloured façades and even giant rosettes along its flanks.

Avant Garde

The DZ Bank Conference Room, in Berlin, Germany, is a radical architectural sculpture by Frank Gehry. Set within a more conventional building (also by Gehry; 1995–2001), the conference suite is a flowing Avant Garde form that wraps over and around the meeting space to create a truly unique venue in the building's central atrium.

Materials and construction

Brick-clad steel
Built in 1891 to a design by Louis Sullivan, the Wainwright Building, in St Louis, Missouri, United States, is a combination of classical form (the three-part column – base, shaft and capital) and modern construction technique. Beneath the building's terracotta façade is a structural steel frame.

Work-related buildings tend to be large and the construction materials used are generally of a size and scale to match. Stone and brick, then steel and concrete have been favourites in the industrial sector over the past 150 years, while the designers of commercial buildings such as offices, stores and technical institutes have most frequently favoured glass, for its sleek, shimmering appeal.

But for every generalisation, there is always a contrast and architects have often bucked the trend to create standout buildings – factories with glass walls or vast concrete edifices containing office space. The common theme throughout, though, is designs that use materials efficiently because when designing a large work building architects have always had to watch the budget and ensure that they are giving their client value for money.

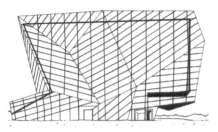

Glass mass

Coll-Barreu Arquitectos designed the
E8 Building (2011), in Vitoria, Spain,
for the expansion of the Alava Technology
Park. The glass and steel façade is a
deconstructed design that seems to
crumple to the ground.

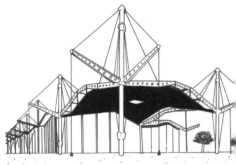

Highly strung steel

Cable-stay construction – steel beams
supported by cables – was used by Norman
Foster in his design for the Renault
Distribution Centre (1980–82), in Swindon,
England. The design looked unique and it
also enabled a 24-m (79-ft) column-free
space within the factory and office building.

Brick beauty

Louis Kahn died in 1974, just as the Indian
Institute of Management, in Ahmedabad,
was completed. He used brick and concrete
as his material palette for every building
on the 24-hectare (60-acre) campus,
creating amazing geometric forms with
the simplest of materials.

Structural wood

Laminating wood has long been practised
but in recent times the ability to build
super-high-strength beams out of laminated
timber has enabled architects to build huge
and beautiful structures out of wood. This
university campus building is totally
supported by laminated wooden beams.

Materials and construction

Now the world-famous art museum Tate Modern, in the former Bankside Power Station (1947–52) on the south bank of the River Thames in central London was designed by Sir Giles Gilbert Scott and began generating power in 1952. Its new owner has added a glazed top floor and capped the giant chimney.

The requirement to build big has always presented special challenges. In the work sector, industrial buildings such as factories, warehouses and so on have compounded these challenges and throughout the 20th century, architects learned more about the properties of materials such as steel and reinforced and prestressed concrete. They worked with technologists to refine them and achieve the optimum performance from them: the results can be seen in some of the massive, columnless spans that have been achieved in the industrial 'sheds' of the recent past. Now, manufacturers had complete freedom to design their production spaces to suit their needs, without having to factor in structural elements such as columns, buttresses or other supports.

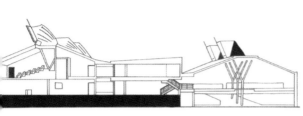

Working green

The Solihull office of architect Arup Associates (2001), features large cowls on the roof that are a combination of skylight and ventilation duct. The architect designed the office building to be super energy-efficient, to showcase its environmental ideals.

Open planning

Today office buildings tend to be open plan, with many people working in the same space. This is a relatively new phenomenon, as offices were generally cellular (everyone having their own tiny room) until the mid-1980s.

Future working

Designed by Will Alsop for the Institute of Cell and Molecular Science, Blizard Building (2005) in Whitechapel, London, houses laboratories and office space in a large, glazed box. Hanging from the ceiling are meeting spaces set within futuristic blobs, the inspiration for which are the cells and viruses on which the scientists work.

Hoover Building

Full metal windows

The small panels of glazing within the banks of windows on the front façade of the Hoover Building are held in place by thin copper-plated frames, which, over time, have turned a patinated green. The frames are indicative of Art Deco design and also hint at a Modernist approach that was still burgeoning in the 1930s.

As you drive along the A40 heading into or out of London, England, you can't help but notice a long, striking white building that looks like something from the 1927 film *Metropolis*. The Hoover Building was designed by Wallis, Gilbert and Partners and built in 1937. It contained a factory and office space for the American vacuum manufacturer.

The design of the building is typical of its time. Art Deco was the architectural style in fashion and architects were often influenced by Aztec and Mayan motifs that came from the artefacts displayed in the 1925 Paris Expo. The layering of the façade on the Hoover Building has wonderful highlights of colour that pick out flourishes and make the building stand out from other industrial architecture in the region.

Making a corner (right)

The curved windows on the corners of the building are thought to have been inspired by Erich Mendelsohn's Einstein Tower in Germany. They feature the same curved head and they contrast wonderfully with the rectilinear decor and form.

Art Deco relief (left)

Even the washrooms in the Hoover Building had style,; the architect cladding the walls in green marble and installing a large circular wash hand basin in the middle of the space.

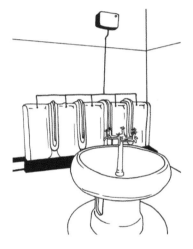

Knock knock (right)

The front entrance to the Hoover Building is a riot of form and colour. The doors themselves are of standard size, but the ironwork surrounding them and the embossed crest at their head make for a stunning entrance.

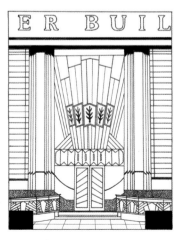

Doors and windows

Adding some fizz
The perfect example of a giant box of a building – a bottling plant no less – that has been pepped up with a little architectural fun is this Coca Cola bottling plant in Los Angeles: it has portholes rather than windows, as part of its 1939 Streamline Moderne design, by architect Robert V. Derrah.

The work building is almost always primarily about function and production; its most important element is the space within – the available area in which to work. The doors and windows are peripheral to the design of the building, apart from their obvious functions of enabling entry and exit, and allowing light and ventilation into the interior.

However, architects make use of all such building components to express a style or genre in the built form; they use these elements to bring design drama to what could be little more than a giant box dubbed 'factory' or 'office'. Doors and windows are probably the most obvious starting point when an architect is looking to add a little flavour to a work building.

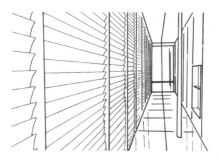

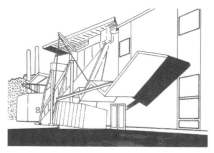

Doubling up

This double-skin glass façade is a very Modern version of the International Style glazed curtain wall. With a walkway between its two façades, the wall construction offers great thermal insulation and has built-in shading, within both double-glazed curtain-walls.

Under the canopy

There are entrance canopies and entrance canopies – and then there is this one at the Funder Factory Works (1988–89) in Austria. The owner of this paper-coating factory wanted to bring drama to the workplace and so employed Coop HimmelB(l)au to design it – and include a Deconstructivist entrance.

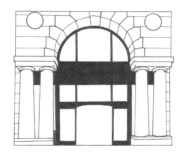

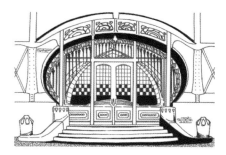

Ironic chic

One workplace that could require a grand entrance is a retail store and here a Postmodern take on classical architecture provides a fashion boutique with a glamorous doorway. The twin pairs of columns are sleek, their styling contemporary but their reference totally classical.

Wonderful contrast

This entrance to what was originally a machine shop at a coal mine in Dortmund, Germany, could not have been more different to the work carried out within. The Art Nouveau doorway is a beautiful combination of organic forms and intricate patterning. The building is now a museum.

Doors and windows

Why design fancy doors and windows for a factory, workshop or other workspace? If business is all about the bottom line, then spending money on beautifying the building is surely unnecessarily extravagant? However, as we all know, image is important in the business world and architects are commissioned to project that image through built works.

Modernist architects and those from the International School could easily combine their designs for doors and windows with the functional aspect of the building, but most genres going before and after chose to glorify them in often non-essential ways. The results, however, were beautiful, as can be seen from the Art Nouveau glazing at the Evian premises in France.

It's in the water

Built in the early 20th century, this building is a part of the industrial heritage of the world-famous bottled water manufacturer Evian, in France. The shape and colouration of the windows indicate an Art Nouveau style, their organic form and even curved glass beautifully constructed into many faceted arches.

Sticking with tradition

This bank building in the United States is a good example of Renaissance Revival architecture of the early 20th century. Traditional and quite reserved, the windows are rectangular and contain several small panes. They sit in a raised classical arch motif, picked out of the stonework.

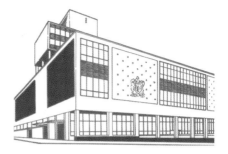

Post, office

Definitely not Postmodern, this International Style post office was opened in Vancouver in 1958. Its massive concrete form is broken up by banks of rectangular windows set within thin metal frames. The contrast between heavy wall and light window frame is typical of the genre.

Modernist welfare

This Christian welfare centre in the United States is a great example of early Modernist design. The large ribbon window in the upper floor is broken up by many vertical brise soleil to limit the amount of sunlight allowed into the building.

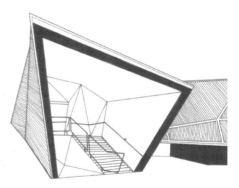

Taking the biscuit

The new museum at the Nestlé Chocolate Factory (2007), in Mexico City, is designed by Rojkind Arquitectos. Its unusual form is accentuated at the entrance, where the building's angular façade opens to reveal a stairway into the Future Modern edifice.

Vitra Fire Station

Hot topic

Looking more like
a giant sculpture than
a place of work, the
Vitra Fire Station, by
Zaha Hadid, was the
building that launched
her now legendary
career as a star architect.
Hadid has courted
controversy since then
with other similarly
extraordinary buildings.

Vitra, a German-based firm that designs and
manufactures contemporary furniture, commissioned
Zaha Hadid to build a private fire station within its Weil
am Rhein premises to protect its entire campus,
following a fire and the realisation that the local
firefighters could not respond quickly enough.

The building, the first built work by the architect, was
completed in 1993. It is an abstract assemblage of
triangular forms, built almost entirely out of reinforced
concrete. Hadid describes the design as 'frozen in
motion; expressing the tension of being alert', as the
firefighters have to be.

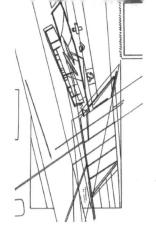

Wall of glass (below)

The long, glazed wall, crowned with a sharpened point of concrete, is another method of projecting movement into the building design, both by offering a reflection of the world surrounding and also in its triangular form.

Bird's eye view (above)

Looking down on the fire station from above you can truly appreciate the abstract nature of Zaha Hadid's design. The building's form and functions are unrecognisable. Instead, the architect has created a sculpture that mirrors her many abstract painted artworks.

Slender steel (right)

These thin steel columns are perhaps an ode to Hadid's Modernist training, so much do they gel with the concrete aesthetic. However, in grouping them together, the architect has created a new dynamic that speaks to the futuristic aspects of her design.

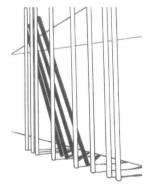

Inside speed (left)

The interior of the building is just as considered as the exterior. The architect has played with lines to create a space that feels constantly ready to explode into action. The form of the shelving and the handrail to the stairs project the idea of motion and speed.

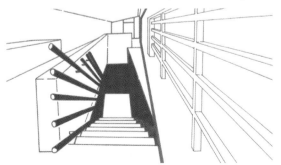

Ornamentation

Art in store

How to make your storefront stand out! The Schlesinger & Mayer department store (1899–1904), in Chicago, United States, was designed by Louis Sullivan in the Chicago School style. This integration of new technique often combined with floral patterning and sculpture is an offshoot of Europe's Art Nouveau style.

Some might say that ornamentation on a work building is a superfluous extravagance that need not be applied, and they'd be enthusiastically applauded by those who follow the Modernist school of thought. But for architects taking a different path, the ornamentation – the inclusion of stylistic flourishes – is as much part of architecture as the functional requirements that make a building work efficiently for its inhabitants.

Architects designing to styles such as Art Nouveau and Postmodernism created work buildings that possess a certain swagger, that extra something that makes them stand out from the crowd – buildings that when we look back on them today give us pleasure through their clever, often witty design.

Postmodern industrial

Designed by John Outram, this ornamented water pumping station (1986), in the Isle of Dogs in London's Docklands, is a wonderful example of Postmodernism in the industrial sector. The coloured bands of brickwork and extravagant column capitals turn a dull building into an architectural spectacle.

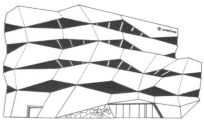

The future fancy

European cell phone provider Vodafone commissioned Barbosa & Guimaraes Arquitectos to design its Portuguese headquarters in Oporto (2008) and the firm came up with this undulating concrete building façade, which is stunning to look at and also structural, making for fewer supports internally.

Modern machine (below)

Aarhus City Hall (1941), the seat of municipal power in the Danish town, was designed by Arne Jacobsen, an architect often better known for his furniture designs. The building is Modernist but includes flourishes like the unusual 'framed' clock tower that elevate it from the mundane.

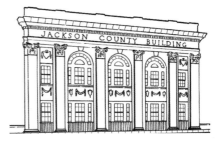

Class is timeless (above)

The Jackson County Court building (1927–28), in the United States, is an understated classical building in the Beaux Arts style. Its brick façade features a false frontage of stone cladding that includes pilasters and window bays with sculpted white stone reliefs.

Introduction

Avant Garde attraction
The Bilbao Guggenheim Museum (1997) in Spain will always be remembered as Frank Gehry's coming of age. Clad in titanium panels, the swirling sculpture of a building is world famous, and it set a course followed by Gehry in many buildings to come.

Cultural buildings come in many shapes, sizes and types, and for these reasons you would imagine that architects have a good deal of latitude when they are designing them. However, just as with an industrial or educational building, there are many requirements for cultural buildings – many must-haves for each specific construction.

Of course, the specific use of the building must be accommodated – stage and seating must be provided in a theatre, naturally lit space in a gallery, an area for storage of artefacts in a museum – while logistical elements have to be considered, including the safe entrance and exit of visitors and deliveries of materials.

That said, the cultural building is often intended to be a celebration of the arts or artefacts: it should be a statement building. The architect is called upon to design something that is not only functional but also

a landmark that visitors will remember. The challenge is one that has in the past pitched architect against building user. Even the great Frank Lloyd Wright came in for some flak for his design of the New York Guggenheim. The building's curved interior walls and sloping ramp gallery were derided by artists who said they were unsuitable for displaying paintings. Lloyd Wright stood his ground, however, stating that artists were lucky to have such a building and that its design would elevate the paintings to a level that was on a par with the architecture.

Many other cultural building designs have been altered or watered down at the insistence of clients and user groups, some for the better, some not. However, the chance to design such a building still attracts many architects, who vie for the opportunity in open and invited architectural competitions. The resulting buildings are some of the most exciting architectural spectacles of the modern era.

Art Deco redo
An Art Deco edifice that was once a flour mill in the city of Gateshead, England, has been renovated (1992–2002) by Ellis Williams Architects and it is now a premier art gallery called the Baltic Centre. This imaginative reuse is unusual for a cultural building, but entirely practical: the wide, open spaces of the flour mill make good galleries.

Archetypes

Renaissance Revival
Built to help workers
learn about the new
industrial mills that
were being constructed
in the area, and to inject
culture into their lives,
Mechanics Hall, in
Worcester, Massachusetts,
was erected in 1857. It
housed a concert hall
and library. Its superb
acoustics make it one of
the United States' top
concert halls.

Cultural buildings have been being designed and built
almost as long as people have been making art of one
kind or another, and collecting artefacts from nature
and society. As such, cultural buildings – museums,
galleries, theatres, movie theatres, opera houses,
pavilions and so on – have been built in almost every
architectural style, right from the times of ancient
Greek architecture to the present day. This proliferation
of styles has given architects a spectacular 'pattern
book' of ideas that include such historical architectural
landmarks as Rome's Colosseum, Tzistarakis Mosque
in Athens (now part of the Museum of Greek Folk Art),
the Natural History Museum
in London and the Prado
Museum in Madrid.

The challenge that architects
have when designing a modern
cultural building is creating
architecture that is as inspiring
as these historic edifices,
while remaining true to their
design ideals.

Beaux Arts

Three glorious wrought iron crowns top the Princess Theatre (1885–86), in Melbourne, Australia. The glamour of this Beaux Arts building is still evident today: its rooftop balustrades are adorned with stone urns while golden lions look out from spots above the ornate pediment that sits high above the main entrance.

Art Nouveau

Teatro Faenza (1924) is the oldest movie theatre in Bogota, Colombia. The building's wonderful front façade features stylised crests that hint at Art Deco styling but the circular decoration around the main door smacks of the more fluid style of Art Nouveau.

Arts and Crafts

Scotland Street School Museum in Glasgow was designed by Charles Rennie Mackintosh as a school in 1903. The building's austere design is set off by two cylindrical towers that house the main staircases. Today, the building is a major architectural tourist attraction.

Modernist

Edens Theater in Northbrook, Illinois, United States, looked highly futuristic when it was built in the early 1960s. Its skyward-pointing roof made it stand out in the suburban neighbourhood. Designed by Perkins + Will, it was demolished in the 1980s.

Archetypes

The De La Warr
Pavilion (1935) is
an International Style
building designed by
Erich Mendelsohn and
Serge Chermayeff, in
Bexhill on Sea, East
Sussex, England. The
architects won a
competition to design
the building. It includes
a concert hall, library,
restaurant and lounge.

Up until the 20th century the design of cultural buildings – and many other types, too – around the world tended to be influenced by geographical location or the by locally ruling dynasty or political power. However, with the birth of Modernist architecture the first period of globally influenced design began.

Modernist ideals from Europe took hold in the United States, while the aptly named International School was promoted around the globe by eager practitioners. Cultural buildings were often the canvases on which these new architectural ideals were laid out, because in this area of construction architects were allowed more latitude to fulfil their design desires than in other building types.

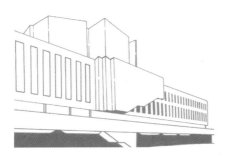

Modern

Alvar Aalto is Finland's most famous
architect and a highly influential
Modernist. His design for Finlandia Hall,
an entertainment and congress building
in Helsinki, was completed in 1971.
Austere white façades are chiselled
through with exacting lines to create
a Modernist masterpiece.

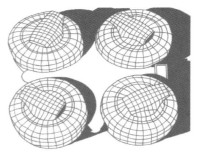

Postmodern

The Hubs (1999) in Sheffield, England,
look like four giant saucepans. Originally
the home of a museum of modern music,
these bizarre Postmodern structures, linked
by a central atrium, are now
occupied by the students
of the nearby Sheffield
Hallam University.

Deconstructivist

Designed by Peter Eisenman, the Wexner
Center for the Arts (1989) is a laboratory
for the exploration of the arts at Ohio State
University, United States. The building
looks like it has been disassembled and
stacked in pieces on the ground, a classic
Deconstructivist statement.

Future Modern

Metropol Parasol (2011) is a giant pavilion
that stretches through a main public square
in Seville, Spain. Designed by J. Mayer H.
Architects, it is used for many cultural
events including concerts. Mayer's design is
familiar and yet otherworldly, and a huge
tourist attraction.

Materials and construction

Marvellous marble
Built as the German Pavilion at the 1929 International Expo, in Barcelona, Spain, the Barcelona Pavilion was Ludwig Mies van der Rohe's ode to Modernism decked out in marble, onyx and limestone. Mies also designed the furniture for the pavilion, including the now iconic Barcelona chair.

The race towards Modernism and the spread of new industrialised techniques encouraged architects to be creative when it came to materials and construction methods, and in cultural buildings they had projects of a size and complexity to be able to experiment.

Every material was used and styles or genres were often fused in grand architectural statements, some of which were pretty hard for the public to understand at the time of their completion. Additionally, since large public projects were often seen as matters of pride for their commissioning government bodies, money was lavished upon new buildings – giving architects more leeway to use the most extravagant and expensive materials on offer.

Stone and brick (below)

Beaux Arts in style and constructed from stone and brick, the Virginia Museum of Fine Arts, United States, was completed in 1936, at a time when other cultural buildings were being designed to ultra-Modernist ideals. The style illustrates the continued love of classical buildings by many in the United States.

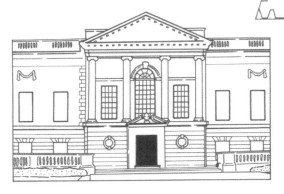

Modernist plan (above)

The layout of the East Wing (1974–78) of the National Gallery of Art, in Washington, D.C., United States, is radical in all aspects. While completely impractical, the design is thoroughly Modernist and daring in its use of triangles to create dynamic spaces and form.

Concrete couture (right)

Sydney Opera House (1958–73), in Australia, is probably one of the most famous buildings in the world. Its beautiful curved roof forms seem so delicate and yet they are constructed from precast concrete ribs, or arches, and finished in ceramic glazed tiles.

Materials and construction

Oak bending

The Downland Gridshell (2002) at the Weald and Downland Museum, United Kingdom, is a latticework of green oak laths that were assembled flat and then slowly bent into the shape of the building. Designed by Edward Cullinan Architects and Buro Happold, the framework is unique and yet low-tech – each joint fixed together using a simple plate and four bolts.

The cultural building in the modern era is akin to the religious one in earlier times – it has come to encapsulate the aspirations of a region or nation. Its designer is encouraged to be expansive and experiment with construction methods in order to make it unique. Take, for example, the Sydney Opera House (page 173) or the Weald and Downland Gridshell (below): the architects of both have taken material science to new levels with their imaginative designs and as a result created buildings that are instantly recognisable and memorable.

These buildings do not follow a trend but set a new one – they represent a triumph of design and of material and construction innovation.

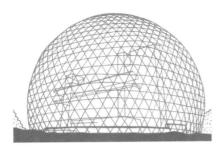

Expo success

The Montreal Biosphere was designed by Buckminster Fuller for the World Expo of 1967. It is a geodesic dome – a curved structure created using a tubular steel frame made up of hundreds of connected equilateral triangles.

Raising the roof

The roof over the Great Court at the British Museum (1997–2000) is an undulating glass and steel structure that stretches over the 0.8 hectare (2 acre) space, making it the largest covered courtyard in Europe. Designed by Foster + Partners, the roof includes 1,656 pairs of glazed panels that are each unique due to the form of the roof.

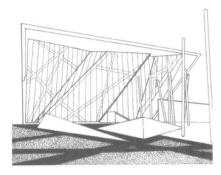

Structurally sound

Architect Daniel Libeskind is renowned for his imaginative use of structure. The Bord Gáis Energy Theatre (2010) in Dublin, Ireland, has a lopsided exposed steel superstructure that has been emphasised to create a drama all of its own.

Captivating cloth

A glass-fibre-covered tensile fabric, stretched over a steel ladder frame creates a unique form and a hard and durable material with which Zaha Hadid has created this extension (2013) to the Serpentine Sackler Gallery in London, England.

Pathé Tuschinski Theatre

The Pathé Tuschinski Theatre in Amsterdam is an Art Deco masterpiece, built in 1921 by Polish immigrant Abraham Icek Tuschinski. Designed by Dutch architect Hijman Louis de Jong (who was eventually fired from the project by Tuschinski), the theatre has an imposing stone façade that is accented with patinated copper window frames and ornamentation.

Inside, the theatre is plush, its owner insisting that the designers (different from the architect) use an Art Deco theme with 'Jugenstil' influences – the Dutch name for Art Nouveau. The result is a building that oozes luxury even today, and which is still cherished by the city of Amsterdam long after it was built.

An immigrant's dream

Entering the Netherlands virtually penniless, Tuschinski made his name in the cinema business, opening four movie theatres. The Pathe Tuschinski was his pride and joy, and became an iconic city landmark as soon as it was built.

Crazy carpet

The carpet in the foyer of the theatre is 50 m (165 ft) long. Originally woven in Morocco, it was replaced in 1984 when a new carpet was made using the original threads, once again in Morocco. The new carpet was delivered in one piece by Dutch airline KLM.

Elephant motif

The front façade of the building features elephant heads carved from stone. This motif is unusual because it differs from the usual Egyptian decoration favoured by Art Deco designers of the time.

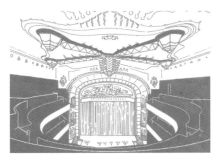

Interior glamour

Horseshoe-shaped – a classical theatre layout – the main auditorium is a combination of Art Deco symmetry (note the lighting) and the flowing organic lines of Art Nouveau design. The result is a beautifully decorated space that was rightly the centrepiece of the building.

Theatre crown

At the top of the building are two towers, each tipped with a copper cupola. The copper has turned green due to patination. Wrought iron balustrades add to the decor, which includes lanterns and stone carving.

Doors and windows

Art Nouveau

The unimaginatively named Municipal House (1905–12) in Prague, Czech Republic, is a concert and opera venue designed in the Art Nouveau style. Above its glamorous main entrance is a mosaic called 'Homage to Prague', by artist Karel Spillar.

The type of building often dictates the specific requirements for doors and windows – think of the differences between an office block and a home. This reasoning applies especially to the cultural building sector, where, for instance, an art gallery requires a great deal of natural light but no direct sunlight, while a theatre has no need at all for natural light in its auditorium. Both buildings, however, want to make a statement with their entrance, so as to attract visitors.

Architects from all eras have had to take all of this into consideration when designing cultural buildings. Then they had to marry the requirements with their style of architecture. The results are often spectacular.

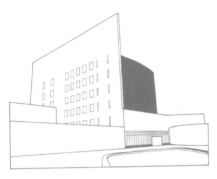

Modernist

Completed in 1979, the John F. Kennedy Presidential Library and Museum (1977–79), in Boston, United States, features a wall of square windows on one side and a completely glazed façade on the other. The contrast is typical of architect I. M. Pei's quirky Modernist designs.

Renaissance Revival

Built in 1900 in Michigan, the Camulet Theatre building has a sandstone portico, or *porte cochère*, at its entrance, which provides covered access to visitors arriving by car, or in the heyday of the building, via horse and carriage.

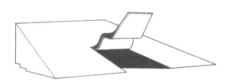

International

The Auditorio Iberapuera (2002–05) is a musical concert venue designed by great Brazilian architect Oscar Neimeyer. The entrance of this International Style structure features a rippling wave canopy that contrasts wonderfully with the triangular uniformity of the building.

Deconstructivist

Daniel Libeskind's extension (2007) to the Royal Ontario Museum is in his trademark style. The entrance is relatively diminutive, cowering under giant, shard-like slivers of windows in this unusual building's lopsided façade.

Doors and windows

Fusion

The Museum de Fundatie, in Zwolle, Netherlands, is a fusion of Renaissance Revival and Future Modern. Its grand entrance (2010–13), complete with colonnade, is presided over by a shimmering, otherworldly ellipse with a giant glazed panel in its side.

As seen on the previous two pages, doors (entrances) and windows are often used to make a grand statement; they are the punctuation points in a building's façade – and are often, indeed, deemed to be exclamation marks! However, the functional requirements of doors and windows cannot be overlooked by architects or users.

The ingress of light is always a consideration – be it allowing in as much as possible, a defined amount or none at all – and swift and safe entrance and exit for building users is of paramount importance, both for a pleasant visiting experience and in case of an emergency.

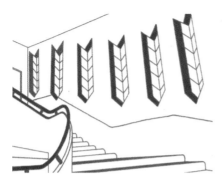

Art Deco (above)

The beautiful chevron-shaped windows on the staircase of the Piccadilly Theatre (1938), in Perth, Australia are more for decoration than functionality. Their form and coloured glass mark them out as Art Deco in style.

Future Modern (below)

The giant glazed portion of the half-ellipse that houses the National Centre for the Performing Arts (2007) in Beijing, China, curves perfectly to match the building. Inside can be seen the mass of steel space-frame required to support the giant window.

Postmodern (below)

A play on ancient classical architecture, the entrance (1981) at the Williams College Museum of Art, in Williamstown, Massachusetts, sees stylised pairs of columns with scrolls that hover above: clever humour in a Postmodern style.

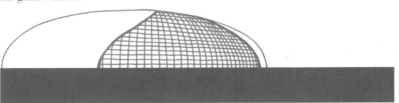

Feature

High Tech hero
Initially the public didn't like the Centre Georges Pompidou but Paris and its people have grown to love the building that has been credited with having turned the art museum world from elitist to accessible.

Home to a library, music research lab and one of Europe's largest modern art museums, the Centre Georges Pompidou is perhaps one of the most famous modern-era museum buildings in the world. It was designed by architects Richard Rogers and Renzo Piano before either had established their now huge firms, and completed in 1977.

The style of the architecture is High Tech, a radical approach that saw the building's mechanical services and elements of the circulation route installed on its exterior, and set within the steel structural frame from which the seven-storey building hangs. The result of this exoskeleton is an interior with no internal columns, making for a wonderfully versatile space.

External service pipes

The tubes on the building's exterior
are colour-coded service pipes: green
for plumbing, yellow for electrical, blue
for air conditioning and red for circulation
and safety.

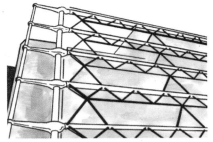

External skeleton

The exoskeleton of the museum is
a trademark of both Richard Rogers and
the High Tech movement. It glorifies the
superstructure of the building and creates
an aesthetic that differentiates the style from
any other genre in the architectural world.

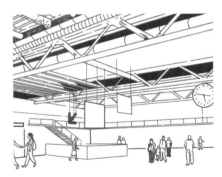

Open interior

The steel exoskeleton supports the massive
lattice beams in the ceiling of the museum.
This structure transfers all loads to the
ground without the need for intermediate
columns, thus enabling the entire interior
to be column free.

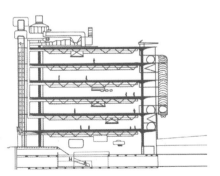

Slice of Pompidou

This section through the museum
illustrates how almost all the circulation
routes between the building's seven floors
are situated on the outside of the building
– see the tubes up the right-hand side of
the image.

Ornamentation

The National Museum of Australia was designed by Howard Raggatt and it opened its doors in 1980. The complex is an intricate swirl of colour and form that combines Postmodern excitement with Deconstructivist chaos.

Decoration is a difficult word for many modern-era architects to use because it goes against many of their beliefs. However, as we've seen in previous chapters some aspects of 20th-century architecture do accommodate a degree of flamboyance.

The cultural sector is perhaps the one most often blessed with a little artistic flourish and museums and theatres are suited to this kind of architectural playfulness. Institutions such as the National Museum of Australia employ radical architects to design iconic landmarks and the results can be extravagant and even difficult to decipher at times. This often leads to a negative public reaction in the beginning but people tend to soften towards these unusual buildings in time and the splashes of colour that they bring are eventually appreciated.

Art Deco

Art Deco design took interior design to new heights early in the 20th century. This chair in the Fox Theatre, Spokane, Washington features an intricate embossed pattern that is typical of the genre, and the exquisite detail that was achieved.

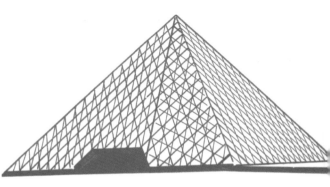

Modernist

The glass pyramid (1989) at the Louvre in Paris is a structure in its own right. It is also a dramatic decoration or adornment to the gallery. Like a giant diamond centrepiece, it attracts visitors who might otherwise pass by the museum with little interest.

Future Modern

The form of the Kunsthaus (2003), in Graz, Austria, is amazing in itself – but the entire façade of the blob-like building is also wired for animated illumination, with thousands of LEDs. Artists can perform lightshows on the side of the museum.

Beaux Arts

Every aspect of the front façade of the Grand Palais (1897) in Paris, France, is adorned with some form of decoration. From the fluting on the pillars to their scrolled capitals, the many statues and the ornate urns, all characterise the building as a fine example of Beaux Arts architecture.

Introduction

Flying High Tech
The International Terminal (1981) at Stansted Airport, England, was designed by Foster + Partners. Its giant tubular steel framework supports a similarly designed roof on minimal internal pillars, allowing for maximum use of the internal space.

While cultural, residential and religious buildings all evolved through the modern era, travel architecture is perhaps the sector that changed the most – in particular the architecture that facilitates mass commercial travel. The 20th century saw a global expansion in railways and shipping terminals: motorised buses began to be seen on the roads as early as 1910, and, in 1939 American Airlines opened the first ever airport lounge for a commercial aviation industry that was still in its relative infancy.

Architects responded to these new challenges in many and varied ways. Railway stations became the cathedrals of the transport world, their train sheds giant arched forms that stretched over multiple tracks, the designs an awe-inspiring combination of architecture and engineering. Bus stations were generally more utilitarian, while airports grew, from

hangars and waiting rooms at the side of airstrips into glorious celebrations of the excitement of flight.

Renaissance Revival and Beaux Arts transport buildings continued a trend set by Victorian architects for railway stations and terminals, the purveyors of newer architectural styles looked to create new built forms for all the transport hubs. Art Deco architects evoked the great ocean-going liners in their works, the buildings being stacked like the ship's bridge and nautical references such as portholes being frequently used. Modernists fell over themselves to champion the very function of these buildings that served the transport types that drove our economies, while Futurists and Expressionist architects – along with today's Future Modernists – challenged convention and looked to wow with transport buildings that defied description and sometimes almost usurped gravity.

Flamboyant Renaissance
Dunedin Railway Station (1906) in New Zealand is a wonderful example of the Flemish Renaissance style. Its dark basalt stonework is contrasted by white stone decoration, making for a dramatic architectural spectacle. It was designed by George Troup.

Archetypes

The archetypal transport building is dependent upon two things, the architectural genre and the type of transport for which the building caters. Whereas residential architecture, for instance, is also often influenced by geographical location, transport buildings tend to be of similar design no matter where in the world they are built.

Transport buildings, by their very nature, tend to be large and – apart from airports – are often squeezed into the very heart of towns and cities. This affects their design: many transport hubs have only one façade on show, while the others are plain utilitarian walls that simply protect the interior from the elements. There are always exceptions, however, as you will see below.

Art Deco

Arnos Grove underground station (1932), in London, England, is a quirky Art Deco building that boasts a striking rotunda above its ticketing hall. The use of brickwork and thin-framed steel windows is typical of public architecture of the era.

Beaux Arts

Gare d'Orsay, in Paris, France, was opened in 1900 as the terminus of the Paris to Orleans railway line. Its stunning Beaux Arts design (internal and exterior) prompted the French government to list the building as an historical monument in 1978 and it is now a museum.

Minimalist

This curvaceous concrete structure is a bus terminal in Casa de Cácares (2004), Spain. It was designed by Justo García Rubio as a single swirl of material, which wraps over and around to form shade and shelter.

Avant Garde

Oriente Station (1998), in Lisbon, Portugal, is a study in Avant Garde metal sculpture. From its winged entrance to the delicate vaulted roof above the tracks, the structure embodies a beautiful simplicity and yet real complexity of design. It was designed by Santiago Calatrava.

Modernist

The sweeping, wing-like design of Washington Dulles International Airport is indicative of the intuitive nature of architect Eero Saarinen's skill as a designer. Utterly functional and yet beautiful at the same time, the airport opened in 1962.

Archetypes

Future Modern

Like some comic book UFO, two giant ellipses form the new main building at Newport Station, Wales. Built in 2010 by Grimshaw Architects and Atkins Engineers, the two organically inspired terminal buildings are linked by a sinuous silver bridge, which spans the tracks.

The elevation of transport hubs from giant sheds into architectural wonders has been expressed in almost every type of modern genre. And, as the 20th century progressed, the role of these buildings changed to better suit our needs (or wants). Where once the requirements were for shelter while waiting for a bus, train or plane, now transport hubs include shops, bars, restaurants, cafes and leisure areas, all catering to consumerist and leisure society.

Additionally, with international travel, security has become an issue and architects have to design in methods of separation and inspection for passengers and luggage. However, while there are multiple elements to consider, the best transport architecture can still be a joy to behold – no matter what its style.

Deconstructivist (left)

Instead of a series of locks, Falkirk Wheel (2002) in central Scotland is a giant boat-lift that has been pared back to its primary engineering elements. Boats are scooped up in a giant tank and slowly raised as the giant cog turns through 180 degrees.

Postmodern (right)

Batumi Airport control tower (2007), in Georgia, is a quirky little piece of Postmodern or even Avant Garde architecture that adds a dash of style to the flat landscape that surrounds it. The architect has combined fun with functionality to great effect.

Renaissance Revival (below)

Simple and yet elegant, the Renaissance Revival building of Diridon Station (1935), in San José, United States, is a lesson in symmetry and style, the high Roman arches setting off the brick building, which is adorned with only minimal decoration at eaves level.

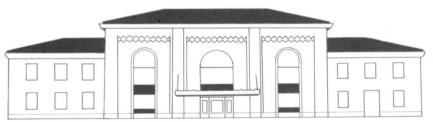

191

Materials and construction

Big buildings demand big solutions and the architects of the 20th century took this to heart when designing transport hubs. Concrete was a great favourite, and still is; meanwhile another industrial material, steel, often became the backbone of a construction project.

That said, there is no shortage of finesse in the transport-building sector. Sculptural forms and intricate detailing have been used hand in hand with giant spans and heavy, load-bearing structures. The results are often awe-inspiring and ultimately accessible to anyone who wants to hop on a bus, boat, plane or train.

Cold cool steel

Vauxhall Cross bus terminal (2004), in London, England, was designed by Arup Associates, the architectural arm of engineer, Arup. The undulating steel bus shelter is a Future Modern intervention at the heart of a gritty part of the city. The folds turn down to form office and waiting space at their ends.

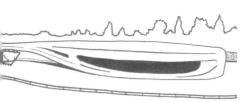

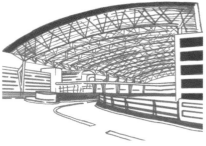

Foaming at the mouth

Whale Jaw (1999–2003) is the name of a bizarre bus stop in the Netherlands. Designed by NIO Architecten, it is formed from expanded foam and then coated in a clear hard epoxy finish. Trying to categorise this structure is impossible.

Glass glass glass

The canopy (1997) above the arrivals and departures drop-off at Portland International Airport is a massive floating glass roof. Suspended on sinew-thin steel rods, the giant glass roof seems to levitate above the ground.

Craftsman style

In the heart of the beautiful wilderness, Yosemite Falls bus stop is an Arts and Crafts response to its surroundings. The shelter uses stone and timber from its surroundings and blends into the environment perfectly.

Concrete sculpture

Now gone, Renfrew Airport terminal (1954) in Scotland was a wonderful example of the achievements of early pioneers of concrete architecture. The Art Deco styling of the building is evident, but the star of the show is the material itself and the forms made from it.

Materials and construction

Breaking new ground

Yokohama International Port Terminal (2002), in Japan, is an architectural wonder projecting out into the harbour. Designed by British firm Foreign Office Architects (FOA), the building is dominated by the walkways and lawned areas on the roof, which serve as a public park in the crowded city.

The sheer scale of some transport architecture is difficult to comprehend – especially when you realise that in some cases before any buildings could be constructed entire new islands had to be built on which to put them. We're talking about colossal architectural projects such as Hong Kong International Airport (1992–98), on the reclaimed island of Chek Lap Kok or Madeira Airport, where a very necessary extension was built to the runway in 2000 on stilts off the side of a hill.

These amazing feats of construction are attributable to engineering genius as much as architectural innovation – in these projects, with the essential support of engineers, architects have pushed the boundaries of what is achievable.

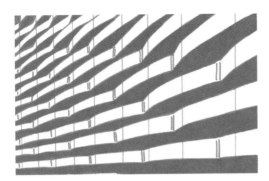

Weaving metal (left)

The train shed (2003) at Worb Station in Bern, Switzerland, is a long rectangular building designed to shelter locomotives that aren't in use. Its design is unique; the architect has used ribbons of stainless steel threaded between vertical rods to create an architectural spectacle.

Cylindrical car park (right)

Ingenhoven Architects designed a multi-storey car park that is cylindrical. The concrete ramps rise like a corkscrew. The walls of the structure are cloaked in thin wooden louvres that disguise the purpose of the building from the exterior.

Environmental design (left)

The roof (c.1980) of Amsterdam Airport Schiphol in the Netherlands is a swathe of green grass. The covering gives great insulation to the buildings beneath and also helps absorb carbon dioxide from the multitude of vehicles that pass around and through the site each day.

TWA Flight Centre

Curvaceous beauty

The curved forms of the concrete airport terminal were completely at odds with other airport hubs of the day. Eero Saarinen's architectural design could be described as Futuristic or even Avant Garde. The building is still widely admired today.

Opened in 1962, the TWA Flight Center was originally the only terminal at New York's Idlewild Airport – now known as John F. Kennedy International Airport. And to this day it is probably one of the most widely recognised terminal buildings in the world.

Architect Eero Saarinen designed the building to evoke flight and the birdlike wings of the building certainly do that. The wings and the rest of the building are constructed in concrete. The building's internal design promotes views of arriving and departing planes through the massive elliptical glazed panels in the front of the building.

Departures board (right)

Perhaps the most elegant departures board and desk ever made, Saarinen's design is a curved, sweeping form that melds both desk and departures board into one sculptural form: this surely influenced current architects such as Zaha Hadid and Jurgen Mayer.

Plan view (left)

The gull-wing plan view of the terminal illustrates its unusual form and the way in which the architect has continued the curvaceous design right through the project. Passengers would embark and return from their journeys via the two stairways at the top of this image.

Main interior space

Giant elliptical windows allow light to flood into the unusually shaped interior of the terminal building. The architect designed sweeping staircases and walkways to allow passengers access to viewing platforms and the bar and restaurant.

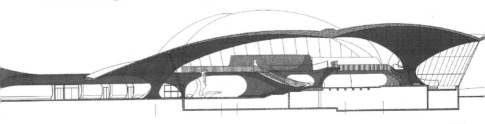

TRAVEL Doors and windows

Artistic architecture
This colourful glazed panel at Miami Airport (2011) adds an element of artistic interest to a large international travel hub. The patterning of the coloured glass mirrors the structural steel of the covered walkway and brightens the walk to the gates on the 'flight' side of the airport.

In this chapter it is perhaps better to think of doors and windows not in their conventional sense – similar to those designed for a house – but more as entranceways to facilitate speedy access and exit, and as means of illuminating gigantic indoor spaces with maximum daylight. Whether the building in question is an airport, a train station or a bus depot, it will likely be dominated by enormous amounts of pedestrian through-traffic: the entrance and the glazed elements are part of an architectural machine designed to ensure that the movement of people and the operations within the building run smoothly. However, this requirement doesn't stop architects from seeking to impress their design skills on transport buildings. Doors and windows are excellent places to punctuate what can often be vast pieces of architecture.

Art Deco

The windows in the main building at Long Beach Airport (1941), United States, look fairly utilitarian at first glance but while those on the upper storey are conventional the horizontal detailing on the ones on the ground floor indicate Art Deco styling.

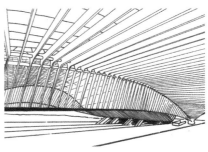

Avant Garde

The entire roof of Liège-Guillemins train station in Liège, Belgium, is glazed. Transparent glass panels span between the slender horizontal roof supports that arc over the entrance area of the rail hub. The design (2009) is by Avant Garde engineer and architect Santiago Calatrava.

Renaissance Revival

Three bays of beautiful, triple-arched windows are the centrepiece at the Centraal Station (1882–89) in Amsterdam. The Renaissance Revival building is a showstopper – but the Modern entrance at its base is a purely functional addition, with no regard for the classical architecture above.

Colonial Revival

Looking more like the arched entrance to an Hispanic ranch house or bar than access to Santa Fe train station (1935), in Pasadena, California, United States, the Colonial Revival building has its roots in Spanish architecture. And just in case you were wondering, it has recently been converted into a restaurant.

Doors and windows

The doors and windows often set the scene for what is to come inside a building – and transport architecture is no different from any other type in this respect. For example, a grand Renaissance or Beaux Arts archway, bordered by colossal columns and crowned with a dramatic transom, almost always signals entrance into a classically inspired train shed that includes a giant arched structure of wrought iron, built at the turn of the century. Conversely, the clinical steel and glass structure of a High Tech airport will most often feature transparent doors that blend with the fully glazed façade. The design is pure function and, inside, the vast departures hall is crisp, clean and free of any unnecessary architectural adornments.

Art Nouveau
This entrance to the Paris Metro is not a door or window but more a signpost directing people into the underground train network. The design is a beautiful example of the organic forms used by Art Nouveau architects early in the 20th century.

International Style

Pure International Style architecture is easy to spot because it is so devoid of any design quirk or decoration. Tulsa International Airport (1928), United States, is an ideal representation of the genre – its flat roof, slender columns and sheets of glazing working in perfect functional harmony.

Modernist

The bar area at the LAX Airport Theme Building, in Los Angeles, has a vertiginous view from windows that lean outwards. The building, designed by Pereira & Luckman in 1961 is a Modernist icon that looks like a spaceship.

Future Modern

The tubular structure that serves as access to flight gates at Shenzen Bao'an International Airport (2012–14) in China features a skin covered in transparent panels, which are interrupted by giant blob-shaped skylights. The design is otherworldly and definitely of the 21st century.

Deconstructivist

The canopies that shield the glazed façade and entrance of Spain's Zaragoza International Airport (2007) from the sun seem disjointed and at awkward angles. This is the intriguing Deconstructivist design of Vidal and Associates Architects, a relatively young firm from Spain.

Waterloo International Rail Terminal

A lengthy feat
At 400 m (1,300 ft) long, the roof of the Waterloo International Rail Terminal is quite a feat of engineering. Additionally, it is curved, snaking either side of the rail tracks that weave a path between many existing and historic buildings in the heart of London.

Costing £120 million, Waterloo International Rail Terminal in London, United Kingdom, was designed by Grimshaw Architects and completed in 1993. It was London's first international terminal, catering to Eurostar trains, which run between London and Paris, and beyond.

The terminal building is predominantly a snaking train shed that acts as a cover to the long Europe-bound trains. It is designed in the High Tech style, a genre for which architect Nicholas Grimshaw is renowned. The 1993 terminal sits next to the much older Waterloo Station, which was built in the mid-19th century in the Beaux Arts style. Today, the two stations act as one and once inside visitors do not know where one stops and the other begins. This is down to an internal upgrade and integration design that removes all trace of the perimeter of the older station.

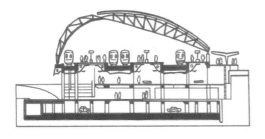

Section through the building (left)

Cut through, the building reveals multiple layers. With a car park at its base, the terminal features two levels of passenger areas, including customs and security areas. Above, at street level, are the platforms and the trains.

Side elevation (right)

The design of the station is dominated by the space-frame roof. However, the majority of the costs incurred in the construction came from the excavation and building of the ancillary services, most of which are buried below the ground.

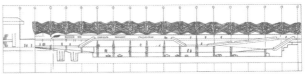

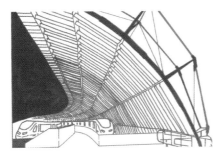

Space frame

The frame that supports the 400-m (1,300 ft) long roof of the terminal is a space frame – a lattice of slender rods and nodes that link together to form a strong framework from which the roof hangs. This design means that there is no requirement for internal columns.

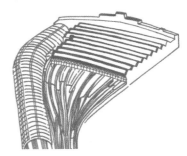

Curved plan view

Much longer than the conventional train sheds of Waterloo Station beside it, the curved roof of the International Terminal is designed to accommodate the longer Eurostar trains, which often park in lines of two on the same track. All the surrounding buildings already existed when the terminal was built.

Ornamentation

High Tech colour

The recently added Terminal 4 (2006) in Adolfo Suárez Madrid–Barajas Airport in Spain is a wonderful example of using colour in architecture. Every structural support column is painted a slightly different hue from the next to create a rainbow effect down the length of the terminal. The design is by Rogers Stirk Harbour + Partners, a practice renowned for its use of bold colours.

Do transport hubs have ornamentation? Of course they do. However, as previously mentioned, ornamentation is often interwoven with the functional requirements of the building, rather than for purely aesthetic reasons.

This doctrine sits well with the Modernist architects who design many of the world's largest and most complex transport buildings. Following the demise of classically inspired styles – Renaissance Revival and Beaux Arts – transport buildings became much more a building type, rather than looking like a glorified manor house or town hall. Architects designed to suit function and the buildings literally changed shape. Along with this came a new aesthetic in which ornamentation often alluded to the function of the building.

Beaux Arts

A last bastion of classical glamour, CFM Railway Station, in Mozambique, is a Beaux Arts station, built in 1916, that has been beautifully preserved. Subtle use of colour amidst the stonework elevates the design, which is crowned with a bronze dome.

Art Deco

Two pairs of statues flank the main entrance of Helsinki Central railway station in Finland. Holding spherical lamps, the stylised figures are part of an Art Deco design by Eliel Saarinen, which was completed in 1919.

Classical eclecticism

This riot of architectural glamour is Centraal Station (1895–1905), in Antwerp, The Netherlands. Multicoloured stonework, gold leaf statues, a clock tower and wrought iron canopy come together in surprising harmony at the city's classically inspired rail hub.

Modern sculpture

This new building (2010) at Queen Tamar Airport, in Georgia, is one of a new breed. Architect Jurgen Mayer shuns conventional ideals to design a building that could be any number of things. What Mayer has done, however, is create a Future Modern icon for the East European country.

Introduction

Brutal schooling
Brutalist or even Postmodern, the Roger Stevens Building, at Leeds University, England, is a dramatic example of how radical architecture is often allowed to flourish in the academic environment. Built in 1970, it is now Grade II Listed and protected as an important asset.

Educational buildings – schools, colleges, libraries and academies, but most of all universities – have always been a favourite with architects as a canvas on which to showcase their skills. Perhaps this is because an architect has had to spend so much time at school in order to reach his goals, or maybe it is because the academic authorities within those schools are often forward-thinking and amenable to the radical architectural ideas that are so often quashed by a commercial world more driven by profit and the bottom line.

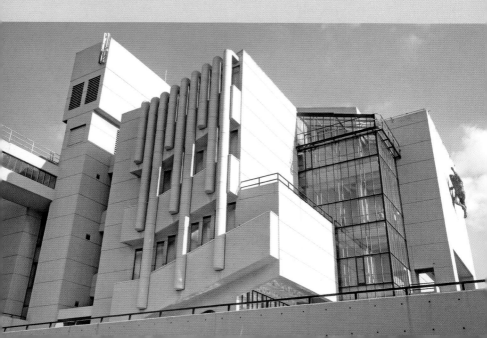

The educational building, whether publicly or privately funded, is designed to a budget and for everyday use, but often has a secondary role – that of attracting students to the university or college. With this is mind, those commissioning new buildings often look to the biggest architectural names to deliver a landmark building that will put the school 'on the map'. And the results do not often disappoint: from the 13th century, when Oxford and Cambridge universities were founded, grand architectural gestures have been commissioned and built in the name of academia. However, many have also fallen by the wayside; their downfall has often been not being flexible enough as buildings to allow the teaching within to adapt with the times. Today architects are tasked with designing educational buildings that not only make a media splash but will also facilitate conventional, new and often unrealised methods of learning, in order that the building will stand the test of time.

This task is an onerous one but architects still jump at it because a standout campus building, a new icon for a university, can change a career and lead to architectural stardom.

Modern American
The Murray D. Lincoln Campus Center (1969–70), at the University of Massachusetts, in the United States, illustrates that Modern/Brutalist architecture was not a British or European quirk. The giant campus building and hotel was designed by Marcel Breuer.

Archetypes

International School
Designed by the father of glass and steel, Ludwig Mies van der Rohe, the S. R. Crown Hall (1950–56), at Illinois Institute of Technology, United States, is all clean lines and minimal frills. The stripped-down aesthetic is International Style at its best.

The educational building has been around as long as humankind has endeavoured to learn, and it ranges from a one-room school house to a university campus that caters for thousands. Of these two extremes, the former tended to possess less architectural glamour purely on account of their diminutive scale; conversely, large university buildings and public libraries were constructed in all manner of lavish classical styles such as Rococo, Baroque, Queen Anne and so on. However, with the beginnings of Modernism a generation of architects were able to design even small-scale schools completely to a style, without the need or desire to lavish time and money on their decoration to suit a design genre. The adage of 'form follows function' applied well to schools of the modern era and architecture thrived in the education sector.

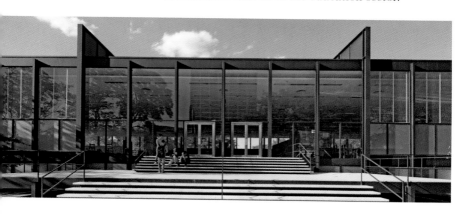

Arts and Crafts

Frank Lloyd Wright believed so much in education that he built his own architectural school, Taliesen (1911), in Arizona, United States. The buildings are wonderfully crafted into the landscape and Lloyd Wright uses large river stones in the walls that speak of his affiliation with Craftsman style.

Art Nouveau

This high school in Germany is typical of Germanic architecture and also the nation's take on Art Nouveau. Small flourishes such as the three Chinese hat roofs, motifs on the end wall brickwork and a wooden cupola allude to a style not often practised in Germany.

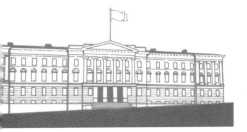

Beaux Arts

Carl Ludvig Engel designed the main building at the University of Helsinki, in Finland, and it was built in the Beaux Arts style in the mid-19th century. It was extensively rebuilt to the original design (1952) after it was bombed in the Second World War.

Renaissance Revival

Normal schools were centres to train teachers in the standards or 'norms' required of them when educating children. Here, the State Normal School Training Building (1904), in San Diego, California, United States, is a demure Renaissance Revival building that keeps frills to the minimum.

LEARNING **Archetypes**

While an architect's brief for any construction project is to design a building that best suits its purpose, with educational buildings another aspect can be added – to design a building that will exemplify the best of your profession and encourage its users truly to appreciate its architectural qualities: after all many of those passing through its halls will one day be influential in their own field.

With this in mind, architects such as Will Alsop have designed standout icons like the Sharp Centre for Design. These are buildings that are simultaneously iconic and practical, buildings that push the boundaries of their genre and construction capabilities of the time. The result is exciting architecture to inspire users and passers-by.

Postmodern

Located in Toronto, Canada, the Sharp Centre for Design (2004) is a unique piece of Postmodern architecture that has become world-famous. Housing classroom space, the building is supported on multicoloured metal posts some four storeys above street level. It is has won numerous international awards.

Avant Garde (above)

Architect Reima Pietilä designed the Tampere City Library, in Finland, and it opened in 1986. He was a proponent of organic architecture – one of the first to promote what is now referred to as biomimicry. The library is best seen from above, when its curvaceous, nautilus shell-like roof can be really appreciated.

Deconstructivist (below)

Designed by Coop Himmelb(l)au, Los Angeles' Modern High School #9 is a grand architectural statement and a school for the performing arts. Its design is unique and obviously Deconstructivist in form: note the disassembled elements and the way in which it leans awkwardly.

Modern (below)

The civil engineering building at Liverpool University (1962) is a good, if uninspiring, example of much educational architecture built in the United Kingdom in the 1960s. Concrete frames with infill panels made for quick construction at a low cost.

Fusion (above)

The business school at Edinburgh Napier University (2004), in Scotland, is a refurbishment of a listed historic building and design of a modern teaching wing, joined together by an outlandish elliptical form that is an atrium space. Designed by architect BDP, it challenges visitors with its bold fusion of styles.

Materials and construction

Metal mayhem
This metal mesh giant, gouged through the middle by a jagged rift, is the 41 Cooper Square (2009), part of the Cooper Union, a college in New York City, United States. Designed by Morphosis, the building is clad in glass, over which is a 'shield' of metal mesh that serves as a sunscreen and an unusual cloak to intrigue passers-by.

The school building is very similar to the office building in many respects: its role is, after all, to house large groups of individuals who will perform repetitive tasks throughout the day. However, while the design of work buildings is usually governed by the bottom line of financial constraints, educational buildings have historically been afforded more leeway, and been designed with higher-quality materials and using more unusual techniques, so attempting to create an air of individuality.

These traits are what we'll uncover in this section – the elements that take the ordinary and make it extraordinary, in the name of architectural excellence. But we won't forget the normal and mundane: the school buildings that most of us experienced as children and young adults.

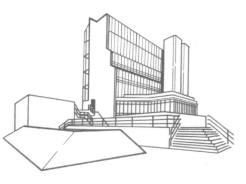

Bricks and glass

The Faculty of History (1968) at the University of Cambridge, England, is a well-conceived building due to its balanced use of two common building materials, bricks and glass. The tranches of red bricks are set well against the glazed sections to create a building that is striking and yet easily 'readable' to visitors.

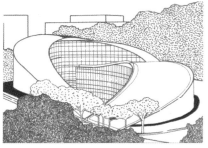

Grass, grass, grass

The sweeping curves that are the roofs of the School of Art, Design and Media (2014) at Nanyang Technological University in Singapore have been planted as lush lawns of grass, and the natural covering makes the form of the roofs even more dramatic than a conventional finish.

It's a steel

Using structural steel to frame views out of its multi-storey windows, the architects of the School of Communication (2007), at San Jorge University, Spain, are getting the best out of a minimal palette of materials: a tactic often used by Modernist architects.

Carved in stone

The Musical Studies Centre (2002), in Santiago de Compostela, Spain, is one of the campus buildings. Hewn from blocks of stone, its exterior gives it an indestructible feel, while inside white walls and roof lights make for a completely different mood.

Materials and construction

Modern amphitheatre
Completed in 1971,
the Florey Building at
the University of Oxford,
England, was designed
by James Stirling. Its red
terracotta tile and glass
form takes on the shape
of an amphitheatre.
The windows overlook
the river and inside are
dormitories for students.

The design of educational buildings is complex, such are the many and varied elements that are required. However, the Modernist tenet of 'form follows function' was a good one to work to and architects in the 20th century embraced the challenge of designing schools, colleges and universities using this mantra.

The designs are most often a combination of multiple buildings linked by covered or open-air corridors. Size, scale and massing depends upon the type of establishment and the amount of land available on which to build. Windows are mostly plentiful and full accessibility has recently become a critical element to build into the design.

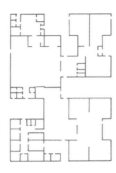

1960s' open plan

This plan view of a school for five-to-eight-year old children shows the first steps towards an open-plan teaching ideal that was born in the 1960s. Classrooms were opened up to create larger spaces in which different activities could be taught simultaneously.

Good wood

The Langley Academy (2008), in Slough, England, was designed by Foster + Partners to replace an ageing secondary school. Its sleek wood-wrapped exterior is a standout feature that brought the academy much attention on its opening.

Prefab sprout

Prefabricated buildings sprouted up all over the United Kingdom following the Second World War to replace damaged property. This school, built of prefabricated concrete panels, is an example of the multi-storey prefab design used around the country from the 1950s through to the 1970s.

Hard lessons

Taking concrete and making it fun. This secondary school in Lisbon, Portugal, rests upon concrete piers with differently shaped holes in their centres – a simple and yet novel idea that elevates the mundane structural element into an area where children will be happy to play and even be inspired by the architect's forethought.

Dessau Bauhaus

Design school

The vast walls of glazing at the Dessau Bauhaus school are indicative of the International Style. Walter Gropius wanted the school to represent the future of architecture and his design was at the forefront of architectural thinking when the building was constructed.

Founded in 1919 in Germany by architect Walter Gropius, the inspiration behind the Bauhaus school was a drive to bring together all forms of art and craft to create totally unified art and design. The Bauhaus movement struck a chord with Modernist architects and had a profound effect upon the genre from the mid-1920s onwards. The school moved from Weimar to Dessau to Berlin during its life, and was governed by Gropius, Hannes Meyer and Ludwig Mies van der Rohe – all three famous architects in their own right.

The Dessau school closed in 1931 as tensions became rife in Germany, preceding the war, and the Nazi Party gained control in the city. It was resurrected

in Berlin for a short while but closed for good in 1933. Today, the school is remembered at its Dessau site, where the buildings that Gropius designed in an International Style while governing the Weimar school still exist.

Sign of the times

The style of font used for the Bauhaus sign is seen today as normal but at the time of its design the lettering was highly Modernist. Its lack of decorative flourishes sets it apart from the classically inspired fonts, depicting a clean, new aesthetic.

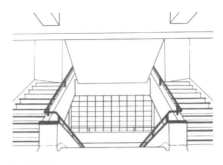

Inside Bauhaus

The interior design of the school is Modernist throughout. Circulation areas such as this stairwell are devoid of glamour but wide, open and inviting due to the influx of natural light – perfectly designed for their function and as such inspired in their form.

Moving parts

The banks of windows in the school open to allow through-ventilation but Gropius didn't want them opened at random and so a clever system of bar and hinges are employed to open and close entire rows of windows in unison.

Plan view

The Dessau school is split into two buildings and three sections, linked by a covered walkway. The Technical School (to the left) houses classrooms and labs; the workshop building is the three-storey section to the lower right; and the single-storey block (top right) is home to the canteen and auditorium.

Doors and windows

The entrance to a place of learning should have some gravitas, shouldn't it? After all, the entrance to a place where you go to expand your mind is important. The entrance to many a classically designed university building is akin to that of a cathedral, but how did Modern architects, predominantly those plying their trade from the 1930s onward, deal with this?

Modern buildings can be as grand as their classical counterparts, but the awe-inspiring nature of their architecture derives more from the impact of the building as a whole than from detailed elements such as the surrounds to doors and windows. Modernists often designed exciting entrance routes towards buildings, while Postmodernists ... well, check out the building below!

Postmodern

This annexe to Storey Hall, at the Royal Melbourne Institute of Technology, in Australia, was designed by Ashton Raggatt MacDougall and built in 1995. Its wacky entrance and unusual window configuration are a Postmodern, almost cartoonish reaction to the classical buildings that neighbour it.

Renaissance Revival

This beautiful arched window at Battle Hall (1909–10), University of Texas, United States, is an example of how Renaissance Revival architecture took its lead from history. The Roman arch and small paned windows are both classical designs that hark back to a time before the United States was established.

Art Nouveau

This series of windows and an entrance to the Glasgow School of Art (1897–1909), in Scotland, illustrate the latitude with which Art Nouveau architects operated in the early 20th century. Look at all the different pane sizes in the windows, and sweeping curve of the stairs to the door.

Modern

Designed by Louis Kahn, the Salk Institute (1965), in La Jolla, California, United States, is the architect's ideal of an intellectual retreat. Kahn researched monasteries in the lead-up to this design and incorporated their influence into his Modernist concrete masterpiece, which includes these 'cells' with simple windows between concrete panels.

Modern Googie

The main campus (1960) at Hope International University in Fullerton, California, is an example of what is termed Googie style architecture in the United States – designs that are influenced by the transport age: cars, aeroplanes and even space travel.

Doors and windows

Deconstructivist
Seattle Public Library, United States, is a Deconstructivist masterpiece, designed by Rem Koolhaas and Joshua Prince-Ramus and completed in 2004. The exterior looks like it has banks of windows below a silver-grid upper façade, but enter within and all that changes. Its skin is glass, encased within a slender framework of steel.

The holes within a building can either define it or be defined by it, especially in the modern architectural era. While they are necessary elements of the functional design, doors and windows have become more than that. Architects that tend towards Minimalism find it challenging to address the requirement for them; while the Postmodernist often sees them as a chance to mock the Modern movement. Ultimately, though, both genres have to deal with them to ensure that their buildings are usable. The door and window are the two most recognisable features of almost any building – or are they?

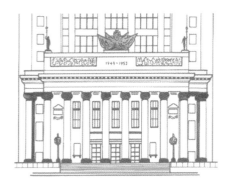

Art Deco (left)

The main entrance of Moscow State University Library (1948–53), in Russia, is a wonderful combination of Soviet style and Art Deco architecture. The sheer monumentality of the building is tempered by the vertical banks of windows and the gold glazed screen surrounding the doorway.

High Tech (right)

Glass blocks fill a series of screens that zigzag around the façade of the Congress Centre (2011) in Zlin, Czech Republic. Designed by Eva Jiricna Architects, the combination of glass and steel is indicative of the High Tech style. The banks of blocks are illuminated at night to glow in gentle shades of pink and purple.

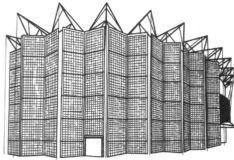

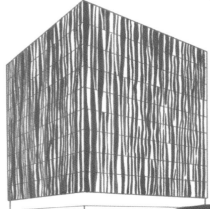

Future Modern (left)

A giant glazed façade of transparent and translucent glass panels forms the wall of this building (2012) at the University of Aberdeen, in Scotland. The doorway itself is lost amidst the disjointed design of the glazed wall that presses almost to the ground.

British Library

British brick

The library is the world's largest in terms of items contained therein: there are more than 150 million, including 14 million books. Four basement levels house most of the pieces, on shelves that if put end to end would stretch 300 km (185 miles).

From the date that architect Colin St John Wilson was awarded the brief to design the British Library it took an astonishing 27 years to complete (1971–98). The project was the largest library to be built in the United Kingdom in the 20th century and it faced numerous challenges, including a change of location and funding crises. However, the building stands today as testament to Wilson's perseverance. Its strict Modernist design has been revered and ridiculed in equal measure, partly because of massive overspend in its later stages.

The building is constructed entirely out of red brick, a material often used by Finnish architect Alvar Aalto. A walled courtyard contains sculptures by Eduardo Paolozzi and Anthony Gormley, and an entrance gate that is larger than many houses.

Entrance

Making a statement from the very beginning is key and the British Library does it with this entrance gateway. Standing four storeys high and featuring the building's name carved in stone, the monolithic red-brick entrance speaks volumes about what is behind it.

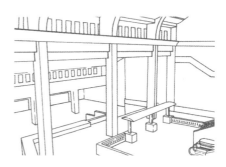

Interior main hall

Coming into the library, visitors enter by the main hall, a gigantic space that includes escalators to an upper level and balconies looking down from the main reading areas. The sloping white ceiling accentuates the building's size and gravitas as one enters into it.

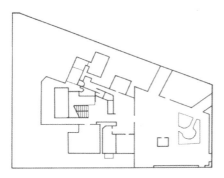

Plan view

The library building itself is shaped similarly to the wedge form of the site on which it sits. The large courtyard creates a processional entrance plaza for the building, which is kept secret from the public gaze by high brick walls.

Rare books archive

Locked away behind glass are 65,000 books and manuscripts that were collected by King George III and gifted to the nation. They are kept in climatically controlled conditions in a six-storey glass vault, dubbed the King's Library.

Ornamentation

Colourful creation

The Cottbus Library (1998–2001) at the University of Brandenburg, Germany, is designed by Herzog & de Meuron. Internally, the architects have used colour with real drama as a means of elevating an already unusual organic design to even greater heights.

Ornamentation in the classical era was an obvious thing: it was a prerequisite of almost all buildings, whether homes or hospitals. However, as architects began to follow the tenets of Modern ideals, ornamentation became a more subtle design element. Gone were the scrolls and pilasters, in favour of stylised brick motifs and simple contrasts in colour or material texture. And this applied to educational buildings as much as any others. Their designers wanted them to be noticed but not at the expense of their genre, and so different tools were used to create standout designs without falling foul of the style in which the architect was schooled.

Art Nouveau artistry

The wonderful organic arch of this window at the Rudolf Steiner School (1901), Antwerp, Belgium, is accentuated by a fresco that sweeps up and around the architectural elements. This was common practice in Art Nouveau design.

Architectural sculpture

The multitude of slender columns that make up the John D. Messick Center (1963), Oral Roberts University, in Tulsa, Oklahoma, United States, stand delicately amidst the bustling campus. Designed by architect Frank Wallace, it is one of a number of his buildings on the site that he envisioned as sculptures.

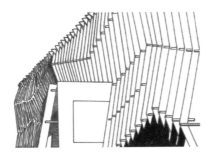

Form as fun

The 2010 lecture theatre at Montan University, in Leoben, Austria, features a façade that thrusts out from the building in an undulating series of fins to create a standout architectural addition to the cityscape – a perfect example of form working as ornamentation.

Beautiful brick

Brickwork is not always thought of as beautiful, or as an artistic adornment, but at Brentwood School in Essex, England, the extravagant multiple-valleyed roof (2011) is twinned with diamonds of raised brickwork picked out of the gables.

Introduction

A grand past
Saltdean Lido (1937–38) near Brighton was once a wonderful example of the Art Deco architecture that flourished in 1930s England. Today, it is a little worse for wear. But the building still has a certain gravitas that the slim lines and curves of the genre lend to buildings such as this.

The term 'leisure architecture' can be used for a whole host of building types: public or private swimming pools, health spas, sports halls and stadia, concert venues, theme parks, hotels, motels and cinemas; all can be considered in different ways venues for out-of-work-activities.

These buildings have evolved significantly over the past century. They have changed due to new philosophies and technologies within their specific field – take the way in which health spas have morphed from tiled bathhouses into holistic treatment centres, or how football stadia have been designed with seating, as opposed to the terraced grounds of the 1930s.

They have also changed with the architectural ideals of the times. The Victorian swimming baths that almost every town in the United Kingdom once had, with an ornate brickwork exterior and wrought iron balconied

changing areas that bordered the pool, have been usurped by high-tech sports facilities that cater to a variety of activities, ranging from swimming to climbing to basketball to five-a-side football. These changes have incorporated Modernist ideals and functional design rationales.

Cinemas, too, are a great example of how building types changed across the 20th century. In the 1930s and 1940s a cinema was most commonly designed along the same lines as a theatre – as a standout building with one large screen and a horseshoe seating arrangement. Jump to the 1990s and multiplexes reigned – ten or more screens housed in warehouse-style sheds. Many of these newer cinemas were designed without an ounce of architectural flair, their remit was to be cheap and cheerful, but certain elements of the leisure sector such as hotels have embraced architecture as a way of attracting paying visitors. Hence we now have the phenomenon of boutique hotels, designed by the world's leading architects and designers.

Triumphant arc
Auditorio de Tenerife (Tenerife Concert Hall) was designed by Santiago Calatrava and built in 2003. Its Expressionist design is unique: the giant arc, which curls over the auditorium, is the largest form of its type to be supported at only two points.

Archetypes

Renaissance Revival
The architectural style of the Plaza Hotel, in Manhattan, New York City, is described as French Renaissance. However, the fact that it was not built until 1907 puts it more than 300 years after that era, and as such, firmly in the Revival style. Still, its classical proportions and ornate gables make for a stunning building.

This section, leisure, is such a diverse area that at times it is difficult to compare individual buildings. However, despite their range of uses, the buildings can still be classified by their architectural genre: their design features are consistent to style no matter what.

That said, the different building types lend themselves to styles in different ways. For instance, a hotel is far more easily designed in Renaissance Revival style than a football stadium; and, due to its era, a lido tends more towards Art Deco than Future Modern. This additional trait – the ability to classify by age due to building type – is fascinating and can only be used in a few cases, where actual building types have gone out of fashion.

Beaux Arts

The Hotel Mercure (1890s), in Lyon, France, is a great example of late 19th-century Beaux Arts architecture. The triple balconies, and three arched windows that are flanked by classical pilasters, take the eye skywards to the crowning arched pediment.

Art Deco

The clock tower and square clock on the Chin Woo Stadium (1953) in Malaysia contrast with the building's cylindrical shape but complement the banks of uniform, thin-framed windows. The patterning of these frames – along with the canopy above the entrance and the flat roof to the tower – point to an Art Deco theme in the design.

Early Modernist

Low-slung structures, white walls and external walkways make the Ace Hotel (1952) in Palm Springs, California, a classic example of early Modern architecture, American style. It fits perfectly into its expansive surroundings, needing no 'extras' to be considered architecturally complete.

International

Looking more like an office building than an entertainment venue, the Queen Elizabeth Theatre, in Vancouver, Canada, opened in 1959. Its lack of any of the pomp of theatres in previous eras, along with the expanses of glass, make it truly International Style architecture.

Archetypes

Deconstructivist
Leaning at an almost impossible angle, the glass entrance to UFA Kristallpalast Cinema (1997–98) in Dresden, Germany, is one element of a cinema complex that is split into chunks by the use of different materials. Designed by Coop HimmelB(l)au, it is a marvellous example of Deconstructivist statement architecture.

As people's lives have changed and society has become more leisure-orientated, the buildings in which we go to enjoy our free time have substantially changed, too. With more people visiting them, attractions such as cinemas and concert venues have had to be made larger – and incorporate elements such as food retail outlets. Similarly, as global coverage of sporting events has increased, the stadia and arenas in which the sport takes place have taken on new importance. While, in the past sports stadiums were simple concrete stands surrounding a pitch or track, now the venue is transformed into an iconic emblem of the team or event.

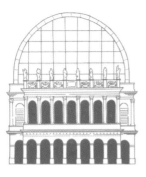

Fusion

Opera Nouvel, in Lyon, France, is named after Jean Nouvel, the architect who reconstructed the opera house in 1985–93 within the shell of a building erected in 1831. Nouvel kept the classical external façade but added below-ground space and the steel and glass-barrel vault roof to create an opera house big enough for the 20th century.

Postmodern

With a sweeping roofline that looks more like a tent than a building, the Peter Hemingway Fitness and Leisure Centre (1968–70), in Edmonton, Canada, was designed by the architect of the same name. The design is a playful and yet stylish take on modern architecture that is lauded by Postmodernists.

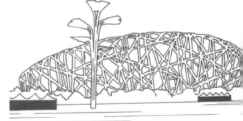

Modern

Built as a basketball arena for the 1960 Olympics, the Palazetto dello Sport in Rome, Italy, was designed by Annibale Vitellozzi and includes a ribbed concrete shell – a construction form favoured by Modernist architects.

Future Modern

Known as the Bird's Nest, Beijing Stadium, China, was the centrepiece of the country's 2008 Olympic Games. Designed by Swiss team Herzog & de Meuron, the stadium is a reinforced concrete structure, wrapped in a 'randomised' steel framework.

Materials and construction

Precious metals

Shimmering in the Spanish sun, Hotel Marqués de Risqual (2006), Spain, is Frank Gehry's ode to Rioja. According to the architect, the titanium ripples that adorn the building reflect pink, alluding to the red wine; silver for the foil shielding the cork and gold, for the ribbons that adorn the bottles.

Looking to make a splash (some quite literally), leisure buildings have often been at the forefront of new or unusual material use and construction methods – all in the name of getting noticed. In the modern era concrete was the first 'new' material, and one that resonated with the architectural thinking of the 1930s onwards. However, since then, many new materials and technologies have enabled architects to further push the boundaries of what we traditionally think of when we imagine building materials and methods. Plastics and fabric have been used; inflatable buildings have popped up, quite literally, and design in the leisure sector has become a competition to see who can develop the most eye-catching building – whether it be a hotel, stadium or public arena.

Fun with fabric (right)

This bandshell, in a park in New York City, United States, is a simple yet ingenious design of slender steel framework over which is stretched an elasticated white fabric. The result is light and ethereal in nature, while being weatherproof for a summer season of performances in the park.

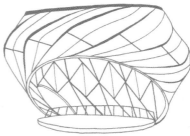

Concrete curling (above)

A wood-framed structure topped with distinctive curved concrete petals, the Don Mills Curling Rink, in Don Mills, Canada, was opened in 1960. Designed by Douglas M. Hall, it was the crowning glory of Don Mills, a planned satellite town.

Inflatable architecture (below)

The Allianz Arena (2002–05), in Munich, Germany is a football stadium clad in inflatable ETFE pillows. The entire façade is also able to change colour, due to LED arrays within each of the pillows. The building was designed by Herzog & de Meuron.

Materials and construction

Aluminium ascent
The Holmenkollen Ski Jump (2008–10) in Norway was designed by JDS Architects. It rises 58 m (190 ft) into the air on a structural frame of steel. An aluminium windscreen and glazing clad the structure, making it comfortable for competitors and the viewing public.

With each material or construction technique comes the opportunity to create a new landmark, a building with a unique feature or look. The industrial aesthetic of concrete is not the only look that Modern-era architects wanted to achieve, and, as time has gone on Modernist ideals have been tempered by the use of all kinds of materials, including traditional (such as wood) and new (such as aluminium), for instance. This ski jump has a certain industrial look but its sweeping form elevates it to be much more than a mere pile of steel and aluminium. The designer has taken rugged materials and made them into something quite beautiful, which is a sporting arena during competitions, and a public viewing platform at all other times.

Wood wonder

Constructed using age-old methods for boatbuilding, the Theatre du Petit Cercle (2004), in Cape Breton, Canada, was designed by Richard Kroeker. Its curved wood walls are not solid, to allow passage of the wind through them.

Bold brick

Phooey Architects designed the Templestowe Reserve Sporting Pavilion (2009) in Melbourne, Australia, for use by the local football and cricket teams. The red-brick design is strong and yet exciting, due to the triangular roof points, which hide solar panels behind.

Sun lovers

Brise soleil are bands of solid material used to deflect the sun from the interior of a building. This yacht club (1940–42) designed by Oscar Niemeyer in Belo Horizonte, Brazil, they integrate with an austere early Modernist design, built predominantly of concrete.

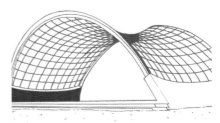

Gorgeous glass

Architect James Carpenter designed this bandshell (2002) for the Schubert Club in Saint Paul, Mississippi. The double curved glass and iron wood structure is delicate and yet strong enough to withstand the spring floods from its river neighbour.

Highbury Stadium

Welcome salute

The cannon crowns a main entrance that is high on Art Deco pomp. Geometric designs are key here: all aspects are accentuated by being picked out with stepped lines and embossed work. Even the lighting is in tune with the architectural design.

Built in the 1930s, the East Stand at Highbury Stadium, home of Arsenal Football Club, England, was part of a redevelopment some two decades after the club first moved to its home in north London. Replacing an uninspiring terrace that stretched the length of the east side of the pitch, the stand is a fine example of how Art Deco architecture was used in sports stadia during the period. Framed banks of windows make the building look more like an office block than a football stadium, the geometric setbacks and details used in the same way that classical pilasters and arch surrounds might be but championing this 'new' style.

The stadium has since been redeveloped as a housing scheme but the East Stand remains (as apartments), and towers over the neighbouring two-storey houses.

Window on the past (right)

Even today, elements such as the side glazing of the stand remain due to their design beauty. These windows were wonderfully designed as part of the Art Deco motif and the redevelopers kept them when building the apartments.

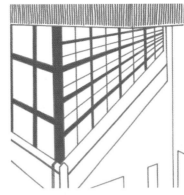

Going East (left)

The football club relocated to a larger ground in 2006 and the original stadium was almost entirely demolished. However, the East Stand and the pitch remain, the former being retained due to its architectural importance.

Club badge (right)

The stylised cannon motif on the sides and front of the East Stand was the football club's emblem. Beautifully picked out, this embossed design has all the hallmarks of Art Deco artistry, from its simple, clear design to the radiating lines that surround it.

Doors and windows

Modern shutters
Designed by Jean Nouvel, the Hotel Le Saint-James, in Bordeaux, France, was built in 1989. Its plain concrete walls are clad in metal grills with simple lift-up shutters at every window opening. The simplicity of the design is its beauty – a Modernist triumph amidst historic vineyards.

Each sub-sector of leisure architecture tends towards a different approach when it comes to doors and windows. For instance, the public sports arena is more utilitarian; its entrance is large and simply defined, its windows purely for letting in light and ventilation. The hotel is more about luxury and occasion and so its door could be an entry into a fantasy; its glazed portions, windows on another world or decorative adornments on a building designed to entertain.

The differing briefs given by clients and public perception of how buildings for different purposes look, represent a challengefor the Modernist architect: in overcoming them, many have created extraordinary buildings of all forms and scale.

Glacial glazing (above)

Rising from the waterfront like the face of a glacier, the Oslo Opera House (2007), in Norway, is all angles and inclines. Its main glazed façade is one of the building's few vertical faces and it contrasts wonderfully with the white stone it is set against, making a statement all of its own.

Art Deco artifact (below)

Opening in 1931, Bush Stadium, in Indianapolis, United States, has hosted baseball, soccer and car racing. Its Art Deco entrance has been witness to the triumphs and losses of thousands of fans but the building is now converted into apartments.

Postmodern giant

The main entrance façade (renovated 1990) of Iowa's Kinnick Stadium is a combination of brick, composite cladding and glass. Its form is a Postmodernist take on Art Deco idealism, the layers of materials, window style and overall grandeur making for a dramatic sight.

Film red

This temporary, futuristic entrance to a theatre in Venice, Italy, was designed for the annual film festival in the city. It is monolithic and angular, using its mass and form as drama for the upcoming films.

Doors and windows

Italian orient

The Oriental Theatre (1927), in Portland, United States, is a quirk of architecture, its name suggesting Asian styling but the building itself being of Italian Renaissance Revival style. The signage looks awkward set against the backdrop of decorated brickwork and row upon row of Roman arches.

Although the Modernists ruled the 20th century, many traditionally schooled architects in this period still looked to classical styles – as have some Postmodernists more recently. This approach delivers the wonderfully detailed entrances and window surrounds that many theatres and hotels still sport today.

However, as technology and materials advanced so, too, did architectural experimentation, and for every 1900 Renaissance or Beaux Arts building that was built, an Early Modernist one was later constructed. The tide was turning and the doors and windows of newer buildings reflected this in their designs.

Leisure buildings followed trends in other sectors and soon the style in vogue was thin frames, large windows and transparent openings. This style has still to be really set aside to this day.

Imagery as architecture (left)

This waveform canopy is an often-seen decorative form on leisure centres and swimming pools. Postmodern in style, it evokes the waterborne activities within, making for an easy reading of the building's use.

Minimalist statement (right)

A simple pair of doors set into a rusted steel lining, the only decoration being the shape of the door handle: this is minimalist decor at its best. The entrance is striking without seeming to give anything away about the interior.

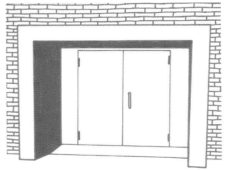

Moving window wall (left)

The Lucas Oil Stadium (2008), in Indianapolis, United States, has a glazed wall on its front façade that can be mechanically retracted to create a giant opening in the building. With architectural advances came engineering ones, too.

Tivoli Concert Hall

Banging the drum

The new entrance building to the Tivoli Concert Hall distinguishes itself from the original building in form, while connecting to the existing by the use of decorative ribbons on its glazed façade, which are similar to the patterning on the façade of the 1950s building.

In 2004 architectural firm 3XN was commissioned to renovate and extend the 1,660-seat concert hall in Copenhagen's Tivoli amusement park. The original building, designed by Frits Schlegel and Hans Hansen, opened in 1956. Its style was a take on Internationalism with quirks to suit the amusement garden surrounds.

The renovation team restored many of the original, but also added a new entrance lobby in the form of a transparent cylindrical drum. This building, which houses the entrance, a lounge area and intermission café, is 700 sq m (7,500 sq ft) in size. The juxtaposition between rectangular concert hall and cylindrical entrance building is 3XN's trick to adding a landmark addition to an already important Danish landmark.

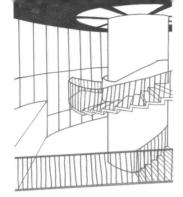

Spiralling ambition

A spiral staircase is the central feature of the new entrance building. Architects have often used staircases to make a statement – think of the processional stairs in many classical buildings.

Glass games

In front of the glazed façade of the entrance building are vertical ribbons. While they twist like paper ribbons, they are metal and serve a dual purpose as decoration and partial shading for the interior of the building during the summer.

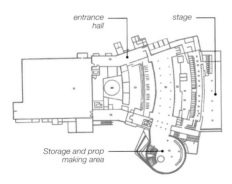

entrance hall — stage

Storage and prop making area —

Bigger picture

The entrance building is just a small part of the concert hall. Seen here at top right, it leads into the main auditorium, with the stage in the middle and the large space to the bottom of the plan serving as storage and the prop-making area.

New old building

The auditorium building has been renovated and its new façade is designed to complement the metal ribbons of the entrance building. The effect is less dramatic due to the scale of the façade and building form.

LEISURE Ornamentation

Colour mad

It's the same shape as any other building of its type, but the Aveiro Stadium (2004) in Portugal has become iconic due to its colourful Postmodern façade. Designed by Tomás Taveira, the interior is as colourful as the external façade – the seating is multicoloured.

The leisure sector contains a good deal of architecture that are seen as landmark buildings and can thrive. As we have discussed, ornamentation has not generally been important for architects in the modern era: it was used at the start of the 20th century, as outgoing classically inspired styles predominated; it was then sidelined for a long period after Art Deco and Art Nouveau. Nevertheless, whatever their style, leisure buildings are there to inspire. Modern designers have used various means to get their buildings noticed, from colour and form to sculptural elements – including nods to the past that sometimes seem out of context.

Architectural sculpture

This fountain, in a park in the United States, is large enough to be considered architecture but in reality it is purely a sculpture. However, it demonstrates how art and design can cross over to create interesting and inspirational built additions to our everyday lives.

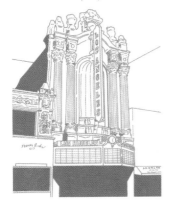

Beaux believers

The giant fluted pilasters, arches and urns that adorn the Los Angeles Theatre, in Los Angeles, United States, are all hallmarks of the building's Beaux Arts design. This wonderfully extravagant example of the genre was opened in 1931 and designed by Charles Lee and Tilden Norton.

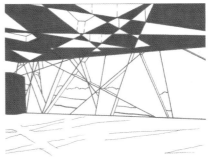

Geometric art

Designed by Toyo Ito and Cecil Balmond, this pavilion in London's Kensington Gardens was the Serpentine Gallery's 2002 summer installation. Its design is an interpretation of the algorithm of a cube as it is rotated, the shapes being solid or transparent to create openings and walls in the pavilion.

Mayan stadium

The Edwards Track Stadium at the University of California is unusual in that it features Art Deco ornamentation that is influenced by Mayan architecture. The stadium was designed by Warren C. Perry and George W. Kelham; it opened in 1932.

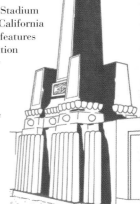

Appendices

Glossary

APEX the pointed top of a gable or pediment.

ARCADE a row of arches.

ARTS AND CRAFTS an international design movement championing traditional crafts, c.1860–1910.

ART DECO a style of art and architecture prevalent in the 1920s, defined by geometric motifs, curvilinear styling and bold colours.

ART NOUVEAU a design style prevalent before WW1, using intricate linear motifs and flowing natural lines.

ATRIUM a sky-lit entrance hall or central court.

AVANT GARDE a group within a style often recognised by experimental or unorthodox methods.

BALUSTRADE a railing with supporting balusters – used on balconies and staircases.

BALUSTER a vertical shaft supporting a rail.

BAROQUE an overtly decorative classical style, c.1600–1750.

BASE the lower part of a column.

BAY the vertical division of a building, often by windows or arches.

BAUHAUS an arts and crafts school in Germany open from 1919-1933. Aslo moniker of architecture influenced by the school's style.

BEAM a horizontal structural support.

BEAUX ARTS a neoclassical architectural style influenced by teachings of the Ecole des Beaux Arts in Paris, c.1850–1910.

BIO-MIMICRY an architectural design which seeks solutions by emulating patterns/ideas from nature.

BOND a pattern of laying bricks.

BOW WINDOW a curved bay window.

BRACE a diagonal support linking a series of uprights.

BRISE SOLEIL a device such as shutters or louvres for shutting out direct sunlight.

BRUTALIST a style of architecture using concrete, the name originating from béton brut ('raw concrete' in French), c.1950s–1970s.

BUTTRESS a mass of masonry built against a wall to reinforce it.

CANOPY a projecting ornamental hood.

CANTED angled.

CANTILEVER an overhanging projection with no support on its outside edge.

CAPITAL the top of a column.

CARTOUCHE a rounded, convex surface, usually surrounded with carved ornamental scrollwork; for receiving a painted or low-relief decoration.

CASEMENT WINDOW a window with hinged panes.

CHAMFER a bevelled edge.

CLADDING an exterior covering.

CLASSICAL pertaining to the ancient Greek and Roman periods.

CLERESTORY a row of high-level windows.

COFFERING a pattern of sunken panels.

COLONNADE a row of columns.

CONCRETE a mixture of cement and aggregate (sand and stones) that dries very hard; it is used as a building material.

CONDOMINIUM apartment building in which each property is privately owned, with the owners sharing ownership of the building itself.

CORBEL a projecting block or capital supporting an arch or shaft above.

CORINTHIAN one of the five Classical Orders.

CORNICE a horizontal projecting moulding, especially the topmost component of an entablature.

COWL hood-like covering to increase the draft from a vent or chimney.

CRUCIFORM cross-shaped.

CUPOLA a small decorative form of dome.

CURTAIN WALL a thin, nonstructural wall in front of a structural frame.

DECK ACCESS a type of apartment block with external corridors running around its perimeter.

DIAGRID gridded network of members that create a structural framework.

DECONSTRUCTIVISM an architectural style of late 20th Century in which designs are analysed and broken down into built elements.

DORMER a window projecting from a roof.

EAVES the part of a roof that projects beyond the wall.

ELEVATION any of the vertical faces of a building, inside or out.

ENTABLATURE the whole of the horizontal structure above the capitals in a Classical Order.

ETFE a fluorine based plastic membrane

EXPRESSIONISM a style in which natural forms are distorted or exaggerated.

FACADE an exterior face of a building.

FANLIGHT a semicircular window over a door.

FANLIGHT a semicircular window over a door.

FORMWORK a temporary structures constructed to hold concrete in position until it is dry.

FRESCO a painting with pigment applied directly onto wet plaster.

FRIEZE a decorative horizontal band, especially the central component of an entablature.

FUSION the act of combining two different styles or forms.

FUTURE MODERN a 21st Century architectural style, using latest forms, materials and techniques.

GABLE the flat pointed end wall of a pitched roof.

GEORGIAN English architectural style of c.1714–1830.

GEODESIC DOME a dome built of short struts which make up multiple loadbearing triangles or polygons.

GREEK the style current in ancient Greece from the 7th to 2nd centuries BCE.

HIPPED ROOF a roof that is pitched at the ends as well as the sides.

HI TECH an architectural style of the 1980s in which elements of high tech industries and technologies were designed into buildings.

INTERNATIONAL STYLE school of architecture emerging in the 1920s and 1930s, defined by form and aesthetics, as opposed to historic styles or social aspects.

INSITU CONCRETE the concrete elements formed and poured on site.

JAMB the vertical part of a door or window opening.

JOIST a horizontal timber supporting a floor or ceiling.

LANTERN a turret or tower on top of a roof or dome to let in light.

LOUVRE any of a series of narrow openings framed at their longer edges with slanting, overlapping fins or slats; often adjustable for admitting light and air while shutting out rain.

MASONRY stone or brick construction.

MODERNIST the architectural style current from c.1920 – late 20th century.

PEDIMENT the gable above a Classical portico; also a gable form used decoratively.

PILASTER a flat column form, usually attached to a wall.

PILLAR a column or pier.

PINNACLE an ornamental structure, usually pointed, on top of a buttress or other structure.

PITCH the slope of a roof.

PLAN a horizontal section or drawing showing the arrangement of spaces in a building.

PLINTH a plain projecting support at the bottom of a wall, column or other upright.

PORCH a partially enclosed space in front of a door.

PORTICO a covered area with a colonnaded front.

POSTMODERN a late 20th Century arts and architectural movement which departed from Modernist dictats.

PRAIRIE STYLE an American architectural style in the late 19th and early 20th centuries.

RENAISSANCE the revival of classical forms and learning in Italy in the 15th and 16th centuries, and in the 16th and 17th centuries in northern Europe.

ROMAN pertaining to ancient Rome, and especially the Roman Empire, 27 BCE–330 BCE

RUSTICATION masonry cut so that the centre of each block projects.

SCAGLIOLA a paste made of pigment, plaster, and glue.

SHAFT the cylindrical body of a column.

SIDING an exterior wall covering made of parallel strips of wood or other materials.

SOFFIT the underside of an architectural structure, such as an arch.

STOREY a level, or floor, of a building.

STRUCTURAL FRAME the construction elements that combine to provide support for the entire building.

STUCCO see Render.

SUBDIVISION land divided into parcels on which multiple properties are built.

SUBSTRUCTURE a part of building constructed below ground.

SUPERSTRUCTURE a part of building constructed above ground.

TENSILE FABRIC a cladding material which includes fabric layer stretched and constantly in tension.

TERRACOTTA a hard, fired clay, brownish-red in colour when unglazed, that is used for architectural ornaments and facings, structural units, pottery and as a material for sculpture.

TESSELATED – tiling or patterning of a surface with repetitious elements with no spaces or overlaps.

TENEMENT large apartment block in which properties are rented by the freeholder.

ZIGGURAT a pyramidal tower, consisting of a number of stories and having about the outside a broad ascent presenting the appearance of a series of terraces.

Directory of Buildings

BUILDINGS TO VISIT

UK/IRELAND

BALTIC CENTRE
Gateshead
www.balticmill.com

BARBICAN
London
www.barbican.org.uk

BORD GAIS ENERGY THEATRE
Dublin, Ireland
www.bordgaisenergytheatre.ie

BRITISH LIBRARY
London
www.bl.uk

BROADCASTING HOUSE
London
www.bbc.co.uk/broadcastinghouse/
visitorinformation

COVENTRY CATHEDRAL
Coventry
www.coventrycathedral.org.uk

DE LA WARR PAVILION
Bexhill on Sea
www.dlwp.com

HILL HOUSE
Helensburgh, Scotland
www.nts.org.uk/property/
the-hill-house

LADY LEVER ART GALLERY
Liverpool
www.liverpoolmuseums.org.uk/
ladylever

IMPERIAL WAR MUSEUM
Manchester
www.iwm.org.uk

RED HOUSE
Bexleyheath, London
www.nationaltrust.org.uk/red-house

ROYAL NATIONAL THEATRE
London
www.nationaltheatre.org.uk

SERPENTINE SACKLER GALLERY
London
www.serpentinegalleries.org

SCOTLAND STREET SCHOOL MUSEUM
Glasgow, Scotland
www.glasgowmackintosh.com/
attraction/scotland-street-school

THE SHARD
London
www.theviewfromtheshard.com/en

TATE MODERN
London
www.tate.org

THE AMERICAS

AGA KHAN MUSEUM
Toronto, Canada
www.agakhanmuseum.org

ART GALLERY OF ALBERTA
Alberta, Canada
www.youraga.ca

BUENOS AIRES HOUSE OF CULTURE
Buenos Aires, Argentina
www.buenosaires.gob.ar

**CATHEDRAL OF OUR LADY
OF THE ANGELS**
Los Angeles, USA
www.olacathedral.org

CONTEMPORARY ARTS CENTER
Cincinnatti, USA
www.contemporaryartscenter.org

EAMES HOUSE
Los Angeles, USA
www.eamesfoundation.org/
eames-house-history

EMPIRE STATE BUILDING
New York, USA
www.esbnyc.com

FALLINGWATER
Pennsylvania, USA
www.fallingwater.org

GAMBLE HOUSE
Pasadena, USA
www.gamblehouse.org

GROPIUS HOUSE
Massachusetts, USA
www.historicnewengland.org/
historic-properties/homes

GUGGENHEIM MUSEUM
New York, USA
www.guggenheim.org

NEW MUSEUM OF CONTEMPORARY ART
New York, USA
www.newmuseum.org

ROBIE HOUSE
San Francisco, USA
www.flwright.org/visit/robiehouse

ROYAL ONTARIO MUSEUM
Toronto, Canada
www.rom.on.ca

**SAN FRANCISCO WAR MEMORIAL
OPERA HOUSE**
Chicago, USA
www.sfwmpac.org

SEATTLE PUBLIC LIBRARY
Seattle, USA
www.spl.org

ST PAUL'S BASILICA
Toronto, Canada
www.stpaulsbasilicaparish.com

UNITY TEMPLE
Oak Park, USA
www.unitytemple.org

WAYFARERS CHAPEL
Rancho Palos Veredes, USA
www.wayfarerschapel.org

EUROPE

BAUHAUS SCHOOL
Dessau, Germany
www.bauhaus-dessau.de/english/
home.html

BILBAO GUGGENHEIM
Bilbao, Spain
www.guggenheim-bilbao.es

CASA MILA
Barcelona, Spain
www.lapedrera.com/en/home

CENTRE GEORGES POMPIDOU
Paris, France
www.centrepompidou.fr/en

CHAPEL OF NOTRE DAM DU HAUTE
Ronchamp, France
www.collinenotredameduhaut.com

HET SCHIP
Amsterdam, Netherlands
https://www.hetschip.nl/en/

GRAND PALAIS,
Paris, France
http://www.grandpalais.fr/visite/en/

GRUNDTVIGS CHURCH
Copenhagen, Denmark
www.grundtvigskirke.dk

JEWISH MUSEUM
Berlin, Germany
www.jmberlin.de

KUNSTHAUS
Graz, Austria
www.museum-joanneum.at/en/
kunsthaus-graz

MUSEE GUSTAV MOREAU
Paris, France
en.musee-moreau.fr

**MONASTERY OF ST MARIE
DE LA TOURETTE**
Eveux, France
www.couventdelatourette.fr

MUSEUM DE FUNDATIE
Zwolle, Netherlands
www.museumdefundatie.nl

NEUE NATIONALGALERIE
Berlin, Germany
www.smb.museum/en/museums-
and-institutions/neue-
nationalgalerie/home.html

PALAU DE LES ARTS REINA SOFIA
Valencia, Spain
www.lesarts.com

PATHE TUSCHINSKI THEATRE
Amsterdam, Netherlands
www.pathe.nl/bioscoop/tuschinski

SAGRADA FAMILIA
Barcelona, Spain
www.sagradafamilia.org/en/

TAMPERE CITY LIBRARY
Tampere, Finland
kirjasto.tampere.fi/english/

TIVOLI CONCERT HALL
Copenhagen, Denmark
www.tivoli.dk/en/haven/spillesteder/
koncertsalen

UFA PALAST CINEMA
Dresden, Germany
www.ufa-dresden.de

UNITE HABITATION
Marseilles, France
www.marseille-citeradieuse.org

VILLA SAVOYE
Poissy, France
www.villa-savoye.monuments-
nationaux.fr

VITRA FIRE STATION
Weil am Rhein, Germany
www.vitra.com/en-cz/campus

ASIA/AUSTRALIA

BURJ AL ARAB
Dubai
www.jumeirah.com/en/hotels-
resorts/dubai/burj-al-arab

JAMA MASJID
New Delhi, India
www.delhitourism.gov.in/delhitourism/
tourist_place/jama_masjid.jsp

LOTUS TEMPLE
New Delhi, India
www.bahaihouseofworship.in

NATIONAL MUSEUM OF AUSTRALIA
Canberra, Australia
www.nma.gov.au

PETRONAS TOWERS
Kualar Lumpur, Malaysia
www.petronas.com.my

ST MARY'S CHURCH
Hong Kong
www.catholic.org.hk

SYDNEY OPERA HOUSE
Sydney, Australia
www.sydneyoperahouse.com

TAIPEI 101
Taipei, Tiawan
www.taipei-101.com.tw

WATANANDA BUDDHIST TEMPLE
Singapore
watananda.org.sg

Index

Index

Index

Acknowledgements

Author Acknowledgement

I would like to thank Jamie Pumfrey, Tom Kitch, James Lawrence and Jenny Campbell at Ivy Press for their patience, assistance and skill in turning my words and picture suggestions into this wonderful publication. Thank you to Jamie Bush for his illustrations. I would also like to acknowledge the authors and contributors to the many books and websites I have used in my research for *How To Read Modern Buildings*. Finally, I'd like to thank my wife, Stephanie, for putting up with me while I struggled through some of the more difficult parts of writing the book.

Author Biography

Will Jones has been writing for architecture and design publications around the world for almost two decades. He is the author of numerous books, including *Modern Architecture in New York* (2002), *Unbuilt Masterworks of the 21st Century* (2009), *The Bicycle Artisans* (2014), and in this series, *How To Read New York* (2011) and *How To Read Houses* (2013).

The publisher would like to thank the following individuals and organisations for their kind permission to reproduce the images in this book. Every effort has been made to acknowledge the pictures, however we apologise if there are any unintentional omissions.

Shutterstock: 2, 4, 5, 7, 11, 12, 14, 16, 30, 38, 42, 44, 46, 48, 52, 54, 56, 58, 62, 64, 68, 88, 92, 94, 96, 106, 110, 126, 127, 128, 130, 132, 134, 138, 142, 144, 146, 154, 167, 172, 180, 182, 186, 187, 196, 198, 200, 204, 206, 210, 216, 220, 227, 228, 232, 234, 246.
Eric Baetscher: 6.
Corbis/Vova Pomortzeff/Demotix/Demotix: 10; Vova Pomortzeff/Demotix/Demotix: 122; 145/Bruce Leighty/Ocean: 124.
Alamy/Nikreates: 18; Peter Moulton: 24; John Gilbey: 26; The National Trust Photolibrary: 40; VIEW Pictures Ltd: 60; Arcaid Images: 80; Edifice: 87; imageBROKER: 112; View Pictures: 120; Arcaid Images: 147; Richard Levine: 148; Grzegorz Kordus: 160; LOOK Die Bildagentur der Fotografen GmbH: 162; B.O'Kane: 164; Loop Images Ltd: 174; VIEW Pictures Ltd: 202; B.O'Kane: 208; VIEW Pictures Ltd: 214; Scott Hortop Travel: 222; Arco Images GmbH: 224; Pick and Mix Images: 226; VIEW

Pictures Ltd: 236; Hemis: 238; imageBROKER: 244.
Getty Images/View Pictures: 32; Philippe Lopez: 100; Robert Landau: 140; Ken Hively: 114; Photograph By David Messent: 184; View Pictures: 188, 190, 192; Barry Winiker: 194; Ullstein Bild: 230; Lars E Andreasen: 242.
Vít Švajer: 36.
Library of Congress: 84, 152, 158, 197, 240.
Flickr/Hiromitsu Morimoto: 50; cjreddaway: 102; Teemu008: 116; Eneas De Troya: 118.
Jimmy Guano: 66.
Raimund Koch/www.raimundkoch.com: 67.
Emma Cross and Jackson Clements Burrows: 74.
Jeremy Atherton: 76.
Michael Locke, Photographer, Los Angeles: 78.
Father Zosimus: 90.
Wikimedia/Janericloebe: 104; Thshriver: 108; Gryffindor: 136; BeyondMyKen: 212; S3335142: 218.
Steve Cadman: 156.
Tony Hisgett: 166.
John Phelan: 168.
Chris Sampson: 170.
Xavi López: 178.
Kevin Rutherford/Creative Commons: 207.